Toby Young

Chris Difford

Jackie Kay

Janet Ellis

Rob D...

...Packham

MY
TEENAGE
DIARY

MY
TEENAGE
DIARY

Edited by Harriet Jaine

BOOKS

his journey from terrified boy to Caped Crusader, so our show tells the origin stories of politicians, poets, authors, journalists, musicians, broadcasters and, yes, comedians.

'What was it that made you what you are?' That's the only question I feel really matters when you're trying to understand someone. It's also a question that, if asked bluntly by even the most charming interviewer, is unlikely to elicit much of a response. It's too personal. But by asking our brave contributors to read from their own accounts of their teenage years with a licence to then probe deeper, that is, in effect, exactly what we're asking. We all know what made Batman become Batman, but what made Terry Wogan become 'Terry Wogan' or Meera Syal 'Meera Syal', and was Chris Packham *always* completely obsessed with wildlife? The answers lie in the pages you now hold, and it remains one of the great pleasures of my life to have uncovered them.

One final note – if you have a child who you believe to be exceptional, please force them to keep a diary. If we're still on the air by the time they're internationally famous, we can book them in an instant – especially if they're a comedian.

Thursday 11
11-354 Week 2 PAYE week 41

Got up quite late, but feel like I got a lot done. Got stage 3 applied for everything going. Scanned photo onto internet which is good. E-mailed a few people from S/P. Got interview for "hostessing" in Japan. Lots of money but a bit scary. Marc left me a message but I think maybe a no-go now! Hayley Hays is coming round with her baby. Feel happier coz i've done some stuff. Have to make sure i go to work tommorow!

Friday 12
12-353 Week 2

Woke up late - its becoming a habit! Went to interview for Quaglino's cat shaydb which i'm very pleased about. Its going to be extremely hard time but @ least i will lose some weight & earn some money & its a nice resturant as well. I'm starting on monday evening which is good as i have this weekend free & can get haircut/ audition on monday! Forgot Kay's - froze my tits off - why oh why was i born blonde?! Got a couple of phone calls offering me 'red cat' work. Got confirmation & drama school.

Saturday 13
13-352 Week 2
sr 8.01, ss 16.18

Going to exhibition with Aurelius! Julia was very good had funky beans last night & woke up feeling very claustraphobic. London was Beautiful & it was great to see J. Mark Rong-on going to Pacific Edge for his birthday this evening, what am i to wear?

Sunday 14
14-351 Week 2
2nd after Epiphany

Andy's ceiling. dinner 7pm.

Day of rest - woke up still tipsy & watched friends video's all day. feel weird about Marc. I am just yearning for some affecta but i knew that he isn't right for me & that he is just settling for me too. Was a weird evening - too hyper yet sad. will miss Andy. Marc was very drunk - got on ok though.

SARA PASCOE

*Sara Pascoe is one of the UK's most successful
comedians. She was born in east London
in 1981. Pascoe's parents separated when
she was young and her dad – a successful
musician – moved away. Before studying
English at the University of Sussex, Pascoe got
a job as a performer in the Millennium Dome.
She became a stand-up in 2007.*

I started writing down my thoughts and grievances from
about seven years old. I had a self-awakening when I realised
I shouldn't be using felt-tips to draw houses and flowers but
to slag off my sister Cheryl. Unfortunately, my sisters are
the reason my earlier diaries no longer exist – we had an
ongoing hiding–discovering–destroying cycle going on with
each other's most precious possessions. If Samuel Pepys had
shared a bedroom with my sisters none of us would have
heard of the Great Fire of London.

My remaining diaries are from my late teens, early
twenties – they still bear the marks of Kristyna's attempts

to sabotage my creativity. The 1999 diary is almost entirely scribbled over in magic marker. It also has 'I HATE KRISTYNA' in the same pen, as this was a trick we used to avoid detection for our crimes. 'It can't be me, it says the person who did this hates me ... it must be Cheryl.'

I didn't reread all the diaries to decide what went in the radio show and the book – it was too much, not because things were particularly sad then, more that I haven't changed. My diaries still read like a teenage girl's: self-hating and angsty one second, then suddenly hopeful and seeing the bright side. I remembered some moments from the extracts very clearly – the fight in the pool club, going to France desperate to be close to my dad. But I had completely forgotten how rubbish I was at being a vegetarian – I'm very embarrassed. I'm so earnest in my writing, I was so desperate for the life I have now and part of me can't help but be impressed that I made it happen. But I wish I could let the younger me know that she'll still cry all the time!

MONDAY 1 JANUARY

2001

Sara is 19.

Woke up in the hotel after a lovely sleep. Didn't feel as sad as I thought I would – I don't think the Dome's closing has really sunk in yet. All my memories of last year are good – I have grown up and don't regret a second of it.

I have stuck to my resolution of being a vegetarian. I think I can stick to it this year!

FRIDAY 5 JANUARY

2001

Felt really sad when I woke up. Had nightmares. Got paid crap from the Dome – cried. Mum agreed to loan me £200. It's horrible to rely on other people.

THURSDAY 11 JANUARY

2001

Got up quite late but got a lot done. Got a copy of *The Stage* and applied for everything going. Scanned photo onto internet which is good. Got interview for 'hostessing' in Japan. Lots of money but a bit scary.

SATURDAY 20 JANUARY
2001

Met Mark for a drink – was going really well – then got a bit awkward. He has got loads of stuff on his mind. He has a beautiful body and is hung like a donkey, but I'm worried we don't really click.

TUESDAY 22 JANUARY
2001

Having a very very ugly day. Skin is minging, hair frizzy, bum fat.

FRIDAY 26 JANUARY
2001

Went out for Mark's work leaving do. Chris and Will attacked virtual strangers for no reason. Was nasty, vicious, and inhumane. What the hell am I doing socialising with people like that? Part of me wonders what I'm doing spending time with such ignorant people, but maybe, in some way, I am educating them.

MONDAY 12 FEBRUARY
2001

Didn't have the money to go to my casting. Spent the day getting rained on going to agencies trying to get a crappy day job. Was very hard – felt like I was selling my soul but I am just so desperate for work now.

FRIDAY 16 FEBRUARY
2001

Drama school audition went very well although I didn't get a place. I was down to the last two and I got some practice with my speeches. Came home and had more funky dreams. Looked in dream book and an ocean wave means I am going to achieve things but I have to work for them.

THURSDAY 5 JULY
2001

Felt down in the morning but then had a brain wave. Have decided to go to university this October. Would make a lot of sense in terms of being able to join really excellent drama groups, study subjects that I love, not have so many money problems and still be able to travel over the summer. Cheered up massively, came back to Romford and had lovely evening.

We join Sara next in October as she is getting ready to go to university.

WEDNESDAY 3 OCTOBER

2001

Tidied and packed stuff. Cried a bit – I like Mark a lot. Spent two hours on train to Brighton reading *The Hobbit*. Saw Halls – mucky but room is nice and big and new. (Haunted apparently!) Forgot to bring duvet/pillow etc. – doh.

THURSDAY 4 OCTOBER

2001

Started sorting room out, bought some cuppa soups and got NUS card etc. Felt pretty crap cos I have no money – spoke to mum and she said, 'You're not going to stick it, are you?' Nice to have support, isn't it? Managed to get duvet and pillow set. Read book and chain-smoked. Spoke to a couple of people in the halls and they all seem very nice.

WEDNESDAY 10 OCTOBER

2001

English induction meeting. Started making some friends. Had audition for *Our Country is Good*. Felt very nervous but it didn't go too badly.

THURSDAY 11 OCTOBER
2001

Busy day today. Two lectures and a seminar. Went to the library (very confusing). Am scared by how much work I am going to have to do on my own. Got part in *Our Country is Good*. Got back, had something to eat (pasta with Philadelphia and Marmite) and went to the computer room.

THURSDAY 25 OCTOBER
2001

Ate pasta with cold beans and read *Lord of the Rings*. Got up late – missed first lecture – made it to the one seminar and then missed second lecture to sort out bank overdraft and paying fees etc. Had rehearsal 6–8pm, went really well.

TUESDAY 8 JANUARY
2002

Woke up with world's worst hormone overload. Felt very very sad and alone. Prospect of spending all day on my own not good. Went to town and signed up direct debits to charities just to have someone to talk to. Went to Sainsbury's and bought tons and tons of shopping – got it all for £30 cos till was broken. Very good. Went home and drank lots of martini. Cried a lot.

SATURDAY 19 JANUARY

2002

Got up late, went to town, spent £40 on books (am going to have to cut down) and bought myself trousers and a top to try and fill empty space inside self. Didn't work. Made spag bol.

FRIDAY 25 JANUARY

2002

Went to St Albans and met Irene for lunch with mum. Had lovely time – ate mushroom stroganoff and drank wine (which really helped hangover surprisingly). On the way home I told mum how much I hate her comments about my nose. Tried to do essay but was too tired.

THURSDAY 31 JANUARY

2002

Woke up today with really really painful chest. Really hurts to breathe and burns when I cough. Went to Asda – bought some basic food and cough mixture etc. Ate loads of Lockets. Chest really hurts though and nothing can make it better. Hung round in room, drank tea and tried to smoke a cigarette. Chest really hurts and nose is running like Linford.

We now join Sara in August 2002. She is going to France to visit her dad, who is playing in a jazz festival.

WEDNESDAY 7 AUGUST

2002

NIGHTMARE DAY! Left for airport. Rain in London meant Liverpool Street underground was closed. Massive panic, tried to make my way through London but missed flight. Didn't get to airport until midnight. Had to sit around waiting – so tired and feeling crap. Never felt so terrible in all my life. Had shakes and was very sick before catching plane. Got to Nice and pottered around. Slept on a beach until 11.30am. Got to the chateau – band were rehearsing. Had lovely food for lunch and dinner and talked to dad.

FRIDAY 9 AUGUST

2002

Everyone is very nice, but I feel uncomfortable and a bit out of place. Watched one concert on the lake. Felt sad and cried. Was strange watching dad on stage. Is hard to write about dad and our conversations as they make me feel so very sad. I'm keeping all the emotions inside.

MONDAY 12 AUGUST

2002

Stayed up very late chatting about the musicians and singers and their interrelationships. Dad was having questions fired from all sides and was like a guru. We sat around and sang songs in harmony – it was delicious and beautiful and I am so sad to go home. Felt like crying at the airport. This week was such an experience for me – especially seeing my dad with his good friends. Feel sick to my stomach with the thought of him leaving this morning. I love him a lot.

Sara is now back at university, starting her second year. She is joined by her family's pet dog, Rusty.

TUESDAY 24 SEPTEMBER

2002

Had burger and chips for tea before remembering that I was a vegetarian.

FRIDAY 11 OCTOBER

2002

Moved into new house. Found out there is no bath. Aargh. Crap not having a bath. I don't think I'll wash any more.

TUESDAY 15 OCTOBER

2002

Was angry cos people used my Dove facial wipes as toilet paper.

MONDAY 28 OCTOBER

2002

Got up and took Rusty for a long walk through park. Was fun
– he chased sticks and ducks and stones. Have fed him lots of
meat and toast.

WEDNESDAY 13 NOVEMBER

2002

Mark cooked dinner (very strange chicken korma with pasta)
but Rusty seemed to like it.

FRIDAY 15 NOVEMBER

2002

Woke up at 10.30 in time to get to seminar. Was good –
alleviated guilt at my being such a lazy bastard. Came home
and read some of Aristotle's *Poetics* for my drama essay. Had
a Bailey's coffee and chatted to Anna. Mark went for a drink
after work and me and Rusty went to meet him afterwards.
Rusty drank a glass of Bailey's and felt very sleepy.

THURSDAY 12 NOVEMBER

2002

There was a disgusting smell. When Rusty jumped on my
bed I thought he had been rolling in poo – he'd actually

had diarrhoea downstairs. Yuk! He tried to wipe his bum
EVERYWHERE!

FRIDAY 13 DECEMBER

2002

Had a brilliant lesson with Alex, really inspiring and
discursive. Got 72 for my essay so was really chuffed. Came
home and found Rusty eating kebab.

WEDNESDAY 25 DECEMBER

2002

Happy Christmas! Actually had quite a nice day. Took the
dogs for a walk and they ran around happily. Saw an owl
flying. Went back and read a bit, then ate a lovely dinner made
by Kris and Cheryl. Fell asleep on the sofa afterwards while
Chicken Run was on. Played a very boring game of Scrabble
and spoke to Mark who was very drunk.

30 MONDAY
WEEK 1 · 364-1

31 TUESDAY
WEEK 1 · 365-0

I went over to Mikes house this)
morning.

SUMMARY OF 1974

There is not much I can say
about 1974 which has not
~~already~~ been said already. We
have ~~had~~ had a power crisis,
two general elections &

1 WEDNESDAY   New Year's Day   Bank holiday, Scotland   rampant
WEEK 1 · 1-364   inflation. I have

mourned three deaths (Becky, Beethoven
& Bob Weinstein) but) I have
made many new friends (Bella,
Michael Heath, Richard Butchins &
the Nick Mills, D.Kelly group). I seem
to have survived through fits of
hypocondria & embarassment. I have
no personal thoughts for 1975 although
I do feel that unless drastic
measures are taken by the goverment,

ROBERT PESTON

Robert Peston is ITV's political editor, presenter of Peston on Sunday, *and founder of the education charity Speakers for Schools. Peston was born in 1960 and grew up in Crouch End, north London, where he attended the local comprehensive school.*

I kept a diary in the early 1970s because that is what a bookish, Jewish, middle-class boy at a north London comp with socialist upwardly mobile parents did. It was like going to the Arsenal or being desperate to buy the latest Emerson, Lake and Palmer album before anyone else. It was pre-ordained.

My mum, in-between making her legendary 'red' rice – whose secret ingredient I am sworn to take to my grave – gave me the Collins two-pages-per-week journal. And I dutifully recorded the spectacularly mundane (dog-walking, chemistry lessons and my consumption of cheesy biscuits), the character-forming (this was the first year that anyone close to me died; and I had almost-proficient snogs) and the prophetic.

Re-meeting that Robert has been surprisingly unsurprising: there I was obsessed with politics and pop music, and a hopeless romantic. In two general elections, which loomed large in our house because my dad was working for the Labour government, I canvassed, though goodness only knows what the householders of Crouch End made of a long-haired underage pipsqueak urging them to vote Labour.

And then there was this on 8 October 1974 from the 14-year-old oracle: 'I saw several of my heroes from the world of eccentricity on the telly tonight (why wasn't I on?).' I am, Robert, I am.

WEDNESDAY 2 JANUARY
1974

Robert is 13.

This afternoon Stewart came over for a game of table tennis. We have developed a system of awarding a certain number of points to the winner of each match we play. This evening I bought dad an *Evening Standard* before eating a supper consisting of ham and chocolate fudge.

THURSDAY 3 JANUARY
1974

This morning I went up to Muswell Hill to have my hair cut. They didn't do a bad job of it, but they charged me £2.50 which I thought was far too much.

FRIDAY 4 JANUARY
1974

This afternoon Tony, Woon and myself went down to Holborn because Tony wanted to go to the market there. The market was closed so we went to Woolworths for a while. I bought a cheap poster of Keith Emerson. We saw a couple of birds there but when we approached them they looked shy so we left them alone.

MONDAY 14 JANUARY
1974

I have just got to go on a proper diet to lose some of this weight. I have been thinking of doing a morning run to see if that does anything for me.

TUESDAY 15 JANUARY
1974

A girl said hello to me this morning. I'm not sure who she was but she lifted me out of my depression, because I thought maybe she liked me.

WEDNESDAY 16 JANUARY
1974

I waited outside the house this morning for a while, to see whether she would turn up again. She didn't.

WEDNESDAY 23 JANUARY
1974

This morning I was feeling very depressed. I must be a maniac as I keep telling myself that I've got no friends and that everyone is against me.

THURSDAY 24 JANUARY

1974

We had a Careers talk during our English lesson. It was worthwhile for some people, but it was a bit worthless for myself. We have a new art teacher. She puts up with anything and she's a bit thick.

SATURDAY 16 FEBRUARY

1974

This evening Richard came over. We talked a lot about moral and personal issues. We drank some beer and ate a cheesy biscuit or two and at 11pm or so he left.

SATURDAY 23 FEBRUARY

1974

I was woken up this morning by the cat meowing outside the front door. Sent off for the Emerson Lake and Palmer tickets. I spent the rest of the day canvassing for the Labour Party with Richard. We walked up and down Stroud Green Road, Crouch End Broadway, Muswell Hill Broadway and Turnpike Lane. It was quite an experience.

WEDNESDAY 27 FEBRUARY

1974

The bloody cat woke me up again. At 4.30pm I got to St Luke's Hall ready for the Labour Party meeting. John Cleese, Eric Idle, Graham Chapman and Michael Palin turned up. After seeing four of the Python members perform once, Mike, Rick and I went down to Drury Lane to see them perform live.

FRIDAY 1 MARCH

1974

I spent most of the day watching the election results come through on the telly. Quite early on this morning it looked like Labour might win with a clear majority. But by 4 o'clock in the afternoon, it was quite evident that, although Labour would gain more of the seats than anyone else, it was only by a margin of 5 from the Tories. In fact, the Tories received more votes than Labour. The election is by no means over as a prime minister has not been chosen yet.

SATURDAY 2 MARCH

1974

At the end of the election Labour got 301 votes and Conservatives 296. We lost our cat for a while. We hadn't seen him all night so after lunch we stuck notices on trees up and down the road.

MONDAY 4 MARCH
1974

Ted Heath has resigned at last and Harold Wilson has moved into 10 Downing Street.

MONDAY 11 MARCH
1974

We had a history test this morning and I got 30/33 which was the highest mark in our class. In biology we measured our lung capacities. In woodwork I have got all my pieces of wood ready for the construction of the spice rack.

THURSDAY 18 APRIL
1974

At 5.30pm me, Dave and Butchins set out for the Empire Pool Wembley and our Emerson Lake and Palmer concert. After taking the wrong train we eventually got there and at 9pm ELP came on. They played a truly amazing 2½ hour set and my ears are still ringing from the noise they produced. We caught the last train home after an encore, and I got home at 1am. My parents were very angry when I got home so late.

SATURDAY 31 MARCH

1974

Dad has got himself a job as advisor to the Secretary of State for Education. This morning I did some homework.

FRIDAY 6 APRIL

1974

Mum went out for the day this morning and Juliet [*Robert's sister*] went over to Tina's house for the day. This meant I was put in charge of Edmund [*Robert's brother*]. At about midday Richard came over and I cooked lunch for all three of us. I burnt the red cabbage we were eating and had a terrible job cleaning the pan. Rick stayed until 9.15 and we whiled away the time playing cards.

TUESDAY 11 JUNE

1974

Took Becky [*the dog*] for a walk. In PE I played cricket in the nets and I also climbed my first proper tree of the year because Ankin hit the ball over the fence. After that I watched this very interesting programme about a Jewish actor's childhood in the East End; little bits of it I found I could half relate to.

SATURDAY 15 JUNE

1974

This morning I went to the Foreign Office with dad, Jul and Ed to see the Trooping of the Colour. I met Shirley Williams and Roy Hattersley there.

TUESDAY 9 JULY

1974

Becky went to the vet again today and it seems that she actually has a tumour (probably on her liver). This afternoon Becky died. She was put to sleep by the vet, but she would have otherwise died very painfully of cancer. Yesterday Becky refused to come into the house. She just sat under a bush, it was as if she had returned to the wild. I look on the death of Becks as the death of a friend rather than that of a pet or a toy. I could talk to Becky like I could talk to no one else. She was a fine companion. I never realised how large a part she played in my life and in the life of the entire family. I cannot write down on paper my real emotions towards Becky. I am just very sad and upset. Bye bye Beckalicker.

SATURDAY 21 SEPTEMBER

1974

I started off this morning by walking up to the Muswell Hill Bejam [*a frozen food store*] to commence my new job. I get approx 1½ hours a day in tea breaks and lunch break. The work I did consisted of filling up freezers, working on the till and stacking cardboard. The guys working in there are fairly sociable geezers. I got paid £3, but I should get a rise next week.

FRIDAY 27 SEPTEMBER 1974

This morning I started my second day's work at Bejam. I unloaded the delivery van with Louie, Kevin, and Terry. I seemed to have started this job at a bad time as I have already witnessed one sacking (that of Richard) and I have been part of a time and motion study. At lunchtime I bought a pair of swimming trunks.

TUESDAY 8 OCTOBER 1974

Dad is beginning to pray for a Tory victory in the election on Thursday, because he wants to give up his job (unfortunately the Tory party seems to want to lose). I just believe in total equality (I call myself an idealistic Marxist). I saw several of my heroes from the world of eccentricity on the telly tonight (why wasn't I on?).

THURSDAY 10 OCTOBER
1974

Today is election day. I went to school equipped with my 'vote for Labour' stickers. In physics we performed an experiment to find the centre of gravity of Great Britain. I watched the Election Special this evening. I drank some wine with mum and dad and went to bed at 2am.

FRIDAY 11 OCTOBER
1974

Labour have won the election with a small majority of three.

WEDNESDAY 16 OCTOBER
1974

I have come to the conclusion that Roy Hattersley dislikes me because when he came over this evening he ignored me. I personally find him a very friendly chap and can't understand why he is not yet in the cabinet.

FRIDAY 18 OCTOBER
1974

I worked all day at Bejam and even did an hour's over time this evening (I even got a free chip from the manager). This evening I went to Bob's party and got myself smashed. No other interesting occurrences.

SUNDAY 3 NOVEMBER

1974

Beethoven [*the cat*] died today, he was run over. The house seems very empty without him. I got the sack at Bejam.

FRIDAY 6 DECEMBER

1974

I discovered today that Bob committed suicide two weeks ago. The main emotional feeling I had when I heard was anger, in that society could force someone to do this. I believe Bob had a very unhappy life, but I still feel it is totally wrong to take one's own life, especially when one is as old (young) as Bob was.

WEDNESDAY 25 DECEMBER

1974

Uncle Willy, Aunty Chunnah, Grandma and Grandpa all came over for our Christmas celebrations today. We had the traditional Christmas dinner of turkey, Christmas pudding etc. I got an electric shaver and a candle-making set from my round the tree presents.

TUESDAY 31 DECEMBER

1974

Summary of 1974

There is not much I can say about 1974 which has not been said already. We have had a power crisis, two general elections and rampant inflation. I have mourned three deaths (Becky, Beethoven and Bob) but I have made many new friends (Bella, Michael Heath and Richard). I seem to have survived through fits of hypochondria and embarrassment. I have no personal thoughts for 1975 although I do feel that unless drastic measures are taken by the government, Great Britain is in for a rough time.

MEERA SYAL

Meera Syal is a writer, actor and broadcaster known for her award-winning coming-of-age novel Anita and Me *and roles in* Goodness Gracious Me *and* The Kumars at No. 42. *Syal was born in Wolverhampton, West Midlands, in 1961. She was awarded a CBE in 2015.*

Growing up a first-generation Asian girl in the middle of white working-class Britain wasn't easy. It was a bit of a lonely existence, and my diary became my friend. A nice, understanding friend who would listen to me ranting about my weight and my crush on Paul Michael Glaser, and who didn't answer back.

It was also a place to practise writing. I was an only child for the first seven years of my life, and I naturally spent a lot of time in my own head. I loved writing short stories and poems and the diary was the testing ground for all that – it was life-saving to discover that the chaos of my inner feelings could be put into words. The diary was the place where I learnt that more or less anything can be made better by writing it down. And, most importantly, it can be made funnier.

Looking back at the diary now, I'm slightly surprised by the amount of self-loathing in there. Thank goodness there wasn't social media back then – I'd have been even more of a mess. On the plus side, I'm impressed that the diary is genuinely amusing. I probably should have been less hard on myself. And I probably should have eaten fewer Chinese takeaways.

THURSDAY 6 MAY
1976

Meera is 14.

I am very depressed about my weight at the moment. It was the netball trials today and I looked really terrible – all the fat hung out over my skirt. My legs are like tree trunks, all brown and rough and my top half wobbles at the slightest movement. And I've practically been starving for 2 weeks!!! Oh! why can't I lose any weight???? Not pigging fair!!!

FRIDAY 7 MAY
1976

Me and Mom and Pops had a Chinese takeaway today! We had sweet and sour chicken which were sort of fritters which I didn't like very much but I ate them anyway. But the noodles, bamboo shoots, water chestnuts, and meat and prawns was lovely!! I ate a lot and put on 2 pounds! Oh well!! I really enjoyed it. Oh and we had chips!!

FRIDAY 14 MAY
1976

I am waging a mental battle within whether to eat a Creme Egg or not. I also wanted to see a *Play for Today* about pop stars but I watched a preview of it with Pops and it was rather dirty. But it looked really good!! If only my parents weren't so reserved I think we'd get on a lot better and avoid all those awkward silences.

SATURDAY 10 JULY

1976

I am bored because I have been in for 2 days and will probably be in tomorrow as well. I want to walk through sun-dappled woods, drink tumbling fresh water from a stream, pick heavily scented wild flowers from lush meadows! It's Angela's party right now. I wonder what they're all doing?

MONDAY 13 SEPTEMBER

1976

I'm really depressed and have been crying because I'm so depressed and fed up about my weight. Firstly, I don't know which scales to follow. At the weigh-in at Judo tonight I was half a stone heavier than on our scales! I've been starving myself for 2 weeks now and I've actually put on weight!! It's not BLOODY FAIR!!! I've got about 5 rolls of flab on my back now, I'm sure they weren't there before! I'm also fed up with Judo. I'm really crap at it and I'm stuck in this stupid competition and I'm going to make a fool of myself by losing all my bouts. Oh yeah. That'll be great. Me. Fat me, being thrown around by Jill or Kathryn and all the lads and little kids laughing at my expense.

BAD FAT POEM
I gaze in the mirror
My brown eyes dilated
My beaky nose wavering with emotion
My butch shoulders bulging with rolls of podge
My stomach bulging flobbering over my waistband
My tears flow freely
Their silvery trail the only thin part of me

SUNDAY 17 OCTOBER
1976

I am quite disappointed because Issy's party was an anti-climax. It had lovely food but I don't think it really got off the ground. The only decent looking boys were Nick Baker and Andy Carter and they were too big-headed for their own good. Reny got drunk, Jenny felt sick, Sue Tenby is a stupid cow who is sex mad and I don't think it was worth paying £1.80 for.

MONDAY 25 OCTOBER
1976

John is really great to talk to at Judo. He is very intelligent, has epileptic fits and reckons God is a spaceman. I have learned a lesson from John. That puny-looking boys aren't necessarily yuk. On the way back from Judo, the brakes in the Mini just conked out. Mom had to leave it in Walsall and get home by bus.

FRIDAY 29 OCTOBER

1976

The reason that I have this great urge to write is that I have to express my love for Paul Michael Glaser who plays Starsky in the *Starsky and Hutch* detective series. It was a really good episode tonight. Starsky was injected with a rare poison by an enemy and he only had 24 hours to live and the way Paul acted was SUPERB and David Soul (Hutch) showed great emotion too. They found the antidote just in time. IT WAS BRILLIANT!! I can't get over Starsky's acting. I really love him. It's not some kind of girly crush but it's a deep deep feeling, almost overwhelming admiration. No actually I REALLY love him!! And I'm not upset or worried that he's old because this makes me feel alive and happy and grateful and many other things that are too beautiful to put down ... There was one episode where his chick was killed in a car accident. I didn't see that one but Jenny said he cried brilliantly the whole way through!!

SUNDAY 7 NOVEMBER

1976

I must realise that he is married or engaged but to be frank, whenever I think of that I feel so desperately jealous! In the last episode when Huggy Bear and Starsky were booked into a hotel where there were lots of pretty secretaries, I felt really jealous!

TUESDAY 9 NOVEMBER

1976

Bad news!! Starsky – I mean Paul – has a steady girlfriend!
She lives in Los Angeles near him and she's really pretty, I
can't even bear to look at the picture in the paper. Just come
back from Dudley Zoo and it's really ruined my mood. And I
was planning to go to America as well. Too late again ...

WEDNESDAY 24 NOVEMBER

1976

Loneliness is a miserable feeling – you feel like you're in a
dark cold place surrounded by walls and all the light there is
comes from a small shaft in the ceiling. Carried along with the
desolate ray of light comes the sound of people laughing and
talking, yet you are all alone.

Loneliness is a wave of self-pity within which you drown
unless you're strong – but I'm not. Sometimes I feel lonely
when I hear the other girls talking about the discos they went
to or the boyfriends that told them they were madly in love.
I know I'm different – and I realise the differences – but
sometimes it's so difficult to keep remembering ... Okay so
I'm a good conscientious Indian girl, I'll work hard and obey
my parents and stay in all the time – well I try anyway!!!
But when I see them trooping off to pubs etc. and trailing
boyfriends behind them, do you think I don't feel anything??
OF COURSE I DO!!! I want to go out and sit in a circle of
friends and tell them about the special boy who thinks so

much of me, who's romantic and humorous and who takes me out everywhere and pays as well!! But, of course, all I can do is sit there and look stupid while they say all these things and mumble something about being Too Tired To Go Out At The Weekend. I HATE IT SOMETIMES!! GOD!!

Yet how can I be sure I'll ever get married? Firstly, I'll need an Indian boy who's fairly westernised and can cope with my weird humour and liberality – and from the boys I've met so far, that seems impossible. And anyway, who would want me? Let's face it, I'm certainly not attractive, everyone keeps telling me how ugly and fat I am – so I suppose I'll end up with some boy I hardly know when I'm about 30 – so I don't think of the future.

I had so many dreams and plans, but they have been shattered and gone …

A Poem. By Me.
Alone, so alone, no spark in the dark, no light to lead me home.
Home, where's home? Nowhere, that's where. A hole where
my soul should be.
Soul? Do I have one? Or am I just a shadow flickering on a wall?
Wall? Whose wall? A castle grim with turrets tall, its
drawbridge up, shut to me while inside revellers laugh and
love.
Love? What's that? Will I ever know the swish of a butterfly
kiss on my lonely neck?
Neck?

Good news. I have got a paper round which is £1·10p per week which is good. Edward bought me lunch today and I owe him 12½p and

I had ...

Price	
A texan 5p	
Some soup 5p	
Some crisps 5p	
A lolly 2½p	
and ods and ends 2½p	
20 p	
Total ↗	

School was a bit better today and it was because I worked a bit

20 p for only 12½p.

harder and didn't talk to much.

The paper round begins at 7·00 and ends at 7·45. I watched Tomkinsons school days it was funny.

TOBY YOUNG

Journalist Toby Young was born in 1963. His book How to Lose Friends and Alienate People *tells of his exploits working on* Vanity Fair *in New York. Latterly, Young has been involved in education, setting up the West London Free School and directing the New Schools Network.*

Crikey! I had forgotten how cringe-inducing my diaries are.

I'm not sure what's worse, the juvenile delinquency or the appalling spelling. I cannot even spell the word 'nick' correctly, which is a shock given how often I talk about 'knicking' things. This reads like the diary of a teenager who is destined to end up in the criminal justice system, and I daresay some of my mates did end up in prison. I'm lucky that I had two parents who did their best to clean up the messes I got into in my later teenage years.

I am conscious that some middle-class parents reading this will worry that, if they send their child to the local comp, he or she will end up like me. Well, let me assure them on two counts. First, state schools are much, much better now than they were in the 1970s. Indeed, the school I went to in London at the age of 11–13 was so poor it was the subject of a *Sunday Times* exposé while I was there! Second, I was a particularly rogue character, destined to end up getting into trouble. I really can't blame the school.

The difference between my own children and myself at their age points to a larger social change, which is that parents tend to keep their kids on a much tighter rein now. Reading these diaries, you get the impression that I was essentially feral, with little or no adult supervision. And I think that's pretty accurate. This led to lots of bad behaviour, as you can see, and I would hesitate to recommend such a laid-back parenting style. But I was forced to learn from my own mistakes. I made so many bad decisions as a teenager that I ended up leaving school at 16 with no qualifications and went on the dole. That proved to be a wake-up call. I realised that if I didn't pull my socks up my life probably wouldn't turn out well, so I went back to school, re-took my O levels and eventually got into Oxford and embarked on a professional career. I wonder if all that would have happened if my parents hadn't let me run wild as a teenager. Maybe. But maybe not.

NB All spelling mistakes in this diary are the author's own …

TUESDAY 6 JANUARY
1976

Toby is 12.

I went school today and I thought it was day one but it was day six and I didn't bring my kit. Luckily I didn't get the slipper because he excepted my excuse. Richard has had his hair cut and I had lunch at Mr Whippy's (ice cream van).

WEDNESDAY 7 JANUARY
1976

Good news. I have got a paper round which is £1.90 per week which is good. Richard bought me lunch today and I owe him 12½ p and I had ...

A Texan 5p
Some soup 5p
Some crisps 5p
A lolly 5p
And odds and ends 5p
TOTAL 20p for only 12½ p.

SUNDAY 18 JANUARY
1976

In the morning Philip Smith came round and we tried to make my train. But I got angry with a piece of flexible track.

After lunch we played in the garden. After school Paul came round and we tied strings to door knockers and hid round a corner and when someone opened the door it knocked on the other door knocker and so on and it was great fun. When Paul had gone I tied some string from one end to the other of the street and watched people get caught up in my spider's web.

TUESDAY 25 MAY

1976

I've decided to make this diary private. I do so many things that you don't know about. I've got girls. I knick things. I swear. I smash windows, I smoke, oh yes I'm a right little tearaway. Today Tom bought me lunch with money he knicked off his dad. He also got some fags for me and Mark. Justin knicked some wrings and necklaces from the jewellers, and he gave me two wrings and a necklace. Justin's really good at knicking.

WEDNESDAY 26 MAY

1976

You know yesterday I was saying Justin was good at knicking? Well today him and Tom got caught, and a police car came round and took down their name and address.

THURSDAY 27 MAY

1976

Mick does a round (paper) about triple the size of mine but he only gets £1.50. School was bad today because Mrs Butler's on my trail about knicking. After school I went to daddy's office party which was on board a ship. You could buy drinks from the bar, even me because it wasn't a licensed bar. I had 2 ciders, 2 babychams, 1 shandy, 1½ pints of schol, and 2 pints of Guinness!! I was (pissed). Pete Black was there and he was also drunk (pissed) on shandys. He must be an alcoholic. Like my aunt.

TUESDAY 8 JUNE

1976

It's really hot nowadays and there has been another heatwave. I hope our country doesn't turn into a tropical country.

I wouldn't mind going out with Julie because there's something about her that turns me on.

FRIDAY 25 JUNE

1976

In the evening I went to Christopher Park's house and I spent the whole evening trying to nick a packet of fags but I didn't. Just before I went to bed I had a cold shower because it was 104 degrees today.

WEDNESDAY 27 APRIL

1977

I can go on skateboarding for the rest of my life.
Skateboarding is an art. Not a dangerous sport which is what
the papers say. It needs a lot of skill, more skill than any
other sport I've tried. Every night I dream about the brilliant
skateboard I'll once have.

SATURDAY 30 APRIL

1977

Yesterday Remi had a get-together and me and Bradley were
sort of fighting over Rowena, but in the end I got her but the
chair we were sitting on wasn't big enough for me to try and
kiss her (even though I would of if I had the chance) and
she was sitting on my lap so all I could get was a bit of a feel.
Man I would like to get more off Rowena. Because I fancy her
pretty badly. I reckon it's a choice between skateboarding or
Rowena because I can either go round with the group or go
skateboarding, and if I go round with the group I stand more
chance of going out with her.

Today I chose skateboarding and went southbound with
Simon.

MONDAY 16 MAY

1977

I'm going to give skateboarding a break for a couple of days because I've done in my head and jaw quite badly.

TUESDAY 17 MAY

1977

At school I nicked an extra bit of lunch. You see, you have an alternative of ravioli or spam fritters. I picked up a plate with spam fritters on and then quickly slipped the spam fritter in my pocket and got some ravioli.

TUESDAY 26 JULY

1977

Today we have moved into Devon, I still can't believe it, it's hard to imagine actually living here, the whole place is a bit of a shambles, everything is dumped everywhere. The air you breathe is much cleaner and fresher and Sasha [*Toby's mother, Sasha Moorsom*] showed me this wild strawberry patch. All the kids here are pretty funny, they all come from well-off middle-class backgrounds and they find the need to show off a great deal.

SATURDAY 10 SEPTEMBER
1977

Today was a pretty full day. In the morning Robert and Pendall called for me and we went down to Aller Park and we were mucking about with a Morris Minor which didn't work, we took it down the hill about three times. Then we were bunging mushrooms at cars and then we were starting up this lawnmower.

WEDNESDAY 15 FEBRUARY
1978

Today I was thinking about the world and how things have changed over the past few years. I should think the world's going to end soon, we've developed too fast too quickly.
We were doin' all right for thousands of years, and then we started mucking about with electrics and factories and we got pollution e.g. for years people have got fish out of a river and had some nice food, but now the sewage has polluted the river and killed the fish. I really do think I'm gonna leave school at 16 especially if I don't get good O level results. I'm going to go around the world and keep on truckin'. But if the world settles down again and reaches a safe level I'm gonna really think about settling down and getting a family. But I'm not going to bring children into the world in its present state. I don't think I should centre my life over the world coming to an end in 1981. But I'm gonna to live my life to the full up to that date.

I find it a little disturbing that so many things—
little things really, have begun to irritate me,
not until — IRRITATE

Case in point; the way Mother and Father always
have everything you do figured out I have
analyzed, critisized, and packaged into a neat
little explanation. They draw on a little
Freud, a little religion, 51% conjecture,
and 34% rationalization. For instance,
I hear it constantly about Gregory— (very
rarely do it to your face;) that way they
don't get any flack. They have an
explanation for everything Gregory was did,
is doing, and will do. I mean everything.
He's usually "trying to prove his
independence," "escaping competing with his
father," "trying to work through his
Eedipus complex," or a thousand other
true (and true) perfect reasons
for what their son does and says. They
never ask him, of course. That somehow
appends their amateur psychoanalysis
pride. It's much more fun to persuade
them while explanations that put them in
a favorable light, & glowing with Christian
tolerance and benevolence.

One example. Mother read some of Gregory's
mail. That, to my mind was clearly unethical
and uncalled for. But what does she say?
It was laying there right out in the open, and
she things that anyone who leaves something
that private and unhidden really wants
her to read it. So she was thoughtly obeying
him. Bullshit. Gregory left that because
he didn't have a person, wrap sure another
by Gestapo inevitably. Her explanation;
for the end, was 100% rationalization.
I leave my mail out all the time, even
my journal is rarely well hidden. Do I

LIONEL SHRIVER

Lionel Shriver is an author whose
breakthrough novel about a school shooting,
We Need to Talk about Kevin, *won the Orange*
Prize. Shriver was born Margaret Ann Shriver
in North Carolina in 1957, the daughter of
a Presbyterian minister and his wife. She
changed her name from Margaret Ann
to Lionel when she was 15, feeling that a
conventionally male name suited her better.

By turns precocious and painfully pretentious, these journal
entries make me alternatingly rather pleased with myself and
desperate to crawl in a hole and die. I used these outpourings
to get a build-up of emotion out of my system, but also to try
on different voices. My first entries were poems, maybe because
my mother wrote poetry. The stilted locutions ('conversations
with that which is three years younger') were attempts to make
experience seem grander. Er – they didn't work.

The 'Tony Shriver' reference cracks me up. I was trying to
ditch 'Margaret Ann' from age eight.

The impulse to record my inner life was born of a pleasure in spinning out words for their own sake; frustration – that I never had an audience who would let me tell my side of things; and a desire to express what I thought, the better to understand what I thought. All those impulses continue to drive my work today. I don't make daily entries, but I still keep a journal.

Reading these mouldy old notebooks, which I hadn't opened in decades, required a particular brand of bravery (I dreaded their being purely an embarrassment) and humility (indeed, I was not nearly as articulate, original or intelligent as I'd have hoped), but also kindness. Forgiveness – for having been a work in progress, a half-formed thing. There's much to be said for nurturing tenderness towards one's own heartbreakingly flawed self, past and present.

After all, my contemporary journal entries are still by turns precocious and painfully pretentious.

SEPTEMBER

1969

Lionel is 12.

Gregory's home [*Gregory is Lionel's older brother*]. You can
tell. He walks in and you are small. The air of importance and
self-confidence enters the room; a well traveled, experienced
man. Man. Funny, very funny. Everywhere I go, 'Are you
Gregory's sister?' I have a strong urge to say, 'No, this is *not*,
this is *Tony Shriver* – look at *me*!' Everyone talks about him.
He's the one who skipped high school and could get into a
state college at sixteen. He must really be smart. But I am just
a stagnant shadow. Just a small child groveling up the glory
left behind by my older brother.

My fingers count out four ...
No, *five*.
Resolutely, another plate removed from
The shelf.
It sure feels funny.

Being suddenly raised king pin
Did have its gratifying moments.
Suddenly, what *I* did was in the spotlight.
A new experience for me.
But I have grown to like it;
He has come back too late.
I enjoy my position.
Enjoyed.
Somehow being second isn't good

Enough anymore.
I don't have a say in the stereo.
The incidentals of my day
Are not frequented by others,
As they used to be.
The tears in Mother's eyes have
Grown moist again.
And guess who's the nucleus of
All conversation.
I fade back to the shadows
From whence I came.

Oh, Gregory!
Love is not gone.
It would simply flourish under
Recognition.
Yes, conversation with that which
Is three years younger may not
Be intriguing, but ought not to be ignored.
I get the distinct impression
Of inferiority in our brief exchanges
Of words. I detest being talked down to.

I do not wish him to go.
I know not what I wish.
I merely realize that things
Cannot stay the way they are.
Every word,
Every motion
Is strained, tense, worried, and uncomfortable.
I feel it.

Gregory feels it.
I don't know,
I just don't know.
I am not ever sure what I'm
Trying to say.
This is just a plea for recognition.
Not a protest.
I'm not being treated *unfairly*.
I simply desire a brother
I can live *with*,
Not in the shadow of.

MARCH

1970

You know, you'd expect a preacher's daughter to be one of the more overly religious people around. But it just *isn't* that way.

I feel like the biggest hypocrite in the world. I go to church every Sunday. I worship in the sanctuary. Stare at the stain glass window, bow my head in prayer, sing the hymns. Say the creed that begins, 'I believe ...' I'm still trying to decide whether there *is* a God. Jesus Christ impresses me as a good guy. Son of God? I don't know. I condemn almost everything this church stands for. But I keep going. To church groups. To fellowships. To meetings. I lie my head off. I even went on a TV program and was given my big opportunity. 'How important do you feel the church is to Jr. High students?' But I evaded and said, 'Well, to some people it is and some not.' Talk about gross.

But like I said before, I'm the daughter of a preacher. This family has had some big disasters in the past two years; I wouldn't want to upset the delicate balance of sanity around here. For human relations' sake, I'll keep going until probably eighteen ... That means every Sunday for four and a half years. That's 134 days of boredom, hypocrisy, and conflict ...

JUNE

1970

[Note from the author: I wrote this entry while lying in bed, listening to my parents argue on the other side of the door.]

GREGORY makes me MAD. HE does things and then condemns me for doing the same thing. He's RUINING me. Trying to run what I do, say, and wear. I can't stand it. Now parents are trying to tell me that their 'reputation is at stake' and I shouldn't wear blue jeans anymore. Their reputation isn't at stake. They're just afraid because of GREGORY. Right now they're talking together about how things were back in their day and now I just do thus and such – Rats, why can't they see they're not on trial? They seem to think they're the ones going to school wearing 'inappropriate dress'. I can hear them in the background talking on about me. How *I* feel, what I'm *really* trying to do, what my *real* motivations are and how I'm just going to have to learn. I have been notified I may NOT wear jeans on Monday. I couldn't wear them yesterday either.

Wow, I'm hearing I don't respect my parents. My mother thinks she's a failure. Gregory thinks I'm immature. I do some of the same things he does and did, and get condemned for it. I buy a certain record and I'm 'going through a stage'. I am just mad, plain old mad. At this *entire* family.

JUNE

1973

Little things have really begun to irritate me.

Case in point: the way Mother and Father always have everything you do figured out. I mean analyzed, criticized, and packaged into a neat little explanation. They have an explanation for everything Gregory ever did, is doing, and will do. I mean everything. He's usually 'trying to prove his independence', 'escaping competing with his father', 'trying to work through his Oedipus complex', or a thousand other tried and true (and tired) perfect reasons for what their son does and says. They never *ask* him, of course. That somehow offends their amateur psychoanalytical pride.

One example: Mother read some of Gregory's mail. That, to my mind, was strictly unethical and uncalled for. But what does she say? It was lying there right out in the open, and she thinks that anyone who leaves something that private unhidden really wants her to read it. So she was simply obliging him. *Bullshit*. Gregory left it out because he didn't have a prison-camp-surrounded-by-Gestapo mentality. I leave my mail out all the time. Even my journal is rarely well hidden. Do I want her to read it? It's beginning to worry me.

But they analyze everybody. With me: I said I don't like little kids. They always smile that secret smile, and finally divulge that it's not children I don't like, but 'the child in myself'. They don't even ask, they tell.

But why don't I like little kids? Because for one thing I think 78.2% of them are evil – just the same percentage as everyone else. I don't like them because they have this angelic reputation, this innocent glow, that is simply deceitful. I don't like them because they cry when their mother leaves, never fail to spread chocolate ice cream all over their bodies, and like to scream for the hell of it at ear-piercingly high frequencies. When they become *people*, that is, when you can see past their dirt covered faces to a little speck of personality, they become tolerable.

But no. All-knowing parents know my mind better. Just the other day I learned to my amazement that I think I am 'above doing the dishes'.

There follows a letter written by Lionel to her older brother, Gregory. Gregory was highly intelligent but troubled. He dropped out of school when he was 14, despite having scored 'genius' in a state IQ test. In later life, Gregory became morbidly obese and then very ill, eventually dying of obesity-related diseases when he was 55 years old.

JULY

1973

Dear Gregory,

The primary reason that I am writing is that I suddenly found within myself the need for a big brother. I think that need has been there ever since you left home, but I was either too ignorant, too proud, or too long without such a brother to recognize it ...

As time rolled on you ceased to be an important part of my life, or more accurately a part of my life *at all*. I remember clearly when I dredged you up from the dregs of my memories the thought would strike: How would I feel if you died? My greatest fear was not of unending sorrow and unbearable wounds, but that I would suddenly discover you were so removed from my life and emotions that your death would not affect me.

During this last year, however, I have found myself more and more identifying with you. I know now what it must have been like for you during these past years. Well, I now know what it's like to be a 16-year-old in the contemporary Shriver family. Believe me, it is a position I would wish on no one.

So I have discovered that I cannot deny you. You are a part of me. Especially in our last two visits I have found that *I love you very much*. And nothing I can do or say can change that.

It is with great fear that I enter the next stage of my life. I now see many of the conflicts you experienced are in my future.

Oddly enough, I think my first battle will be that of religion. Well, anyway, I still have to go to church every Sunday and wear pretty little dresses and mumble all that is put in front of me. I am presently sick and tired of pretending, so as to not rock the boat.

In this letter, I have tried to recognize that I cannot deny you – but that conception has a companion – neither can you deny me.

With more love than I ever know,
Your Sister

(20)

was it was a train the next day (wednesday). At the west african
bank one chap didn't know its dollar exchange rate. I let some
bretons behind the counter at Barclays who told us that on the
night of the killing they didn't see a thing, but next morning
things were bad (one whole trainload was made to get off and
all were chopped). The result was chaos and the trains were
held hostage by the eastern region (service down to one a day),
and the ibos blame + hate britain for it all as the Hausard love
britain and the B. government kept supporting the undemocratic
regium. Stewart + Alain from barbeach drove round the eastern
region due to the anti-british police. The lads at the bank were
waiting for letters from home that had left before us. The food
was typical west african chop yam + banana, basic rice + fish
or meat. The begging is terrible — all the time — all the people.
Oranges 1d, Bananas 2a 1d. Beans 1d a huge portion. The hotel
was very noisy and its estimacies continue all day until 1 pm.
Went mad with joy at the USIS library and on the way home
we were stopped by a peddler who I knocked down to 3/- on
the shell basket (and mick got a python skin down to £2). One chap
stopped us and started to explain about how he was going to wash
his shirt cos it be dirty and then started to take his pants off with the
same intention, we reassured him that we understood. There was
joy in finding pineapples at 1/6 - 2/-, and we gorged. Mick knocked
the guides - Kuma fare down to £2.10.0d and we had to pay £2. 18 for
the train (the ticket man called us to the front of the queue to give us tickets).
The next morning we set off, horace in a towel (one man thinking
him to be a snake). The platform was crowded and we piled up with
bread + bananas. We had to fight for a place (after the panic caused by
its leaving too soon). The singing beggars - breast feeding mammies -
- urinating babies - the long line of squatting urinaters at each stop
- the dug over fields + non existant forest. The people think every

KEN LIVINGSTONE

Ken Livingstone was the first Mayor of London from 2000 until 2008, and head of the Greater London Council from 1981 to 1986. He is, famously, an enthusiast of newts and amphibians, and was born in Lambeth, south London, in 1945.

When I decided to trek across Africa I was 21 and had never left Britain before. That was quite normal in those days when only the very well-off could afford to have a holiday abroad, so I wanted to keep a diary to remind me of this very exciting adventure. I did hope that one day I might be able to publish it but I didn't realise I would have to wait 45 years for that to happen. When I decided to include parts of it in my autobiography and went back to read it, I instantly realised that over half of it was so boring that I could only include the more exciting bits.

Reading it now reminds me of what a different world it was back in 1966 – not just here in London, but even more dramatically in Africa. Half the places I visited wouldn't be safe to go to now but back then the newly independent countries in Africa were filled with optimism for their future, whereas now so many of them are caught up in dictatorships or wars.

If I could go back and give myself advice I would say I should have kept a diary throughout my life; it would have made it a lot easier and quicker to do my autobiography if I had. But I liked spending time with my family a lot more than sitting at a desk writing. But this five-month trip changed my life, and reading about those days now makes me so pleased I went.

THURSDAY 29 SEPTEMBER
1966

Ken is 21.

Calais

We spent the morning packing our rucksacks – they weighed well over 50lbs each!

When we arrived in Calais, it was too late to get a lift, so we had to camp the night. We were watched by some policemen who were very amused when I fell over backwards into a ditch trying to get the tent up.

Girls are very confident here. One who gave us a lift just turned round and said everyone would think Mick was homosexual because of his long hair. I was stunned at her frankness.

The girls are nowhere near as pretty as in London; they also lack mini skirts and it now seems odd not to see girls' knees.

The toilets are very awkward and often lack hand basins. The French don't bother about flies and only flick them away when they get near their eyes or nose.

SATURDAY 15 OCTOBER
1966

Tangiers, Morocco

We took a hotel room after much haggling. Left the light on all night to discourage the bedbugs but still a few appeared.

The Casbah is very dirty, has a large traveller population of self-conscious misfits and real 'don't cares' (they all talk about hash as though you were abnormal not to take it). One Norwegian became the third person to ask me if I was an Aussie because of my accent. The Arabs insistently offer hash or boys or girls or dancing or an illegal exchange rate.

SATURDAY 22 OCTOBER

1966

Algiers

The travellers here all sleep with their money at the bottom of their sleeping bags. The habit is catching and we have become very distrustful. The hostel treats everyone like kids with lights out at 10pm, which is odd because half the people are over 40.

We went to see the botanical gardens where the ponds are full of painted frogs; all males, brown, grey, spotted, striped, fat as butter and don't swim away when we pick them up. The zoo was as bad as Madrid's. A large jam jar with holes punched in the top and stuck down with Sellotape contained a pink horned viper. The attendant said he'd rather I'd put it down.

Things here are as expensive as in Europe and we are still waiting to reach the places where people tell us we can live on a shilling a day. We manage to pass ourselves off as students and get cheap meals (chicken and haricot beans) at the university. One chap told us that the British were hated because there has been no action against Smith in Rhodesia, but that English students are good because they dislike Smith.

THURSDAY 10 NOVEMBER

1966

One of the Aussies has just returned from Colomb Béchar having been halfway through the Sahara. He says the French are still in control of the interior of Algeria and there's much more traffic than he thought. The cars and lorries always stop and there are loads of little villages where people give travellers eleven days' hospitality according to the Koran or something. Apparently all the guff about how hot it is in the day and how little water there is is way off the mark, so Mick and I are now much happier about our prospects of getting through.

Left Algiers on 8 Nov and got a lift to Blida, where we picked up another lift from an old FLN [*National Liberation Front*] member who is now chief of Electricity supply in the Djelfa area.

He drank bottles of beer consistently as we drove through the day and to reassure us that his drinking had no effect on his driving, he stopped the van and with 100 percent accuracy shot a succession of beer bottles out of the sky as we threw them up for him.

We camped last night – our first in real desert – but I was awoken when a large cockroach fell on my face.

SUNDAY 13 NOVEMBER

1966

In Salah.

Is very depressing due to its desolate and grubby nature. Just a few palm trees and a filthy little market with dried meats

and dates all covered with swarms of flies. We camped in the
shelter of a garage as there was a medium-sized sandstorm
for a couple of days. The heat was terrible in the day but we
kept fairly warm at night. Our presence attracted some large
stag beetles, but there was nothing else to be found in the
place. The shops are all identical, they sell three kinds of jam,
sardines, cheese spread and corned beef. We get bread from
a baker's which everyone crowds around at opening time and
pushes and fights to get into (queues don't exist outside of
Britain). Because of the heat we are able to pour corned beef
from the can onto our bread.

THURSDAY 17 NOVEMBER
1966

After we left In Salah, we camped in a flat sandy area
surrounded by sharp cruel mountains in a perfect circle about
seven to ten miles across. There was a small central peak,
which I climbed in the last rays of the sun. When I got to the
top the sun had set. The whole thing was like the surface of the
moon, and I could have been standing in the centre of a crater
... the place was covered in snake tracks.

   The day after that, I had my bad bout of diarrhoea. This
got worse by the hour, until I was passing crystal-clear green
mucus laced with blood, and was too weak to walk. I was
losing weight so rapidly that my watch-band was hanging
off my wrist. As we were at least a day from Tamanrasset, I
didn't think I was going to make it, and lay there thinking, 'I'm
only 21 and I'm going to die without having done anything
worthwhile.'

SUNDAY 20 NOVEMBER

1966

Agades

The town centre has a large depression where everyone goes to defecate while vultures hop around looking for anything edible. All the food has sand in it.

We were twenty-five miles south of Agades when suddenly the car swerved off the road and went chasing after three adult ostriches and about twenty of their young. All the Africans jumped out to catch the young ones. I was chasing after one with an African just in front of me when the ostrich turned round and ran into my feet. As the others that had been caught were destined for the pot I insisted on keeping Horace, as we decided to call him. He is about two feet high to the top of his head and we feed him on banana, tomato, oranges and bread. He walks around at the end of a rope, pecking everything in sight. When we get to Accra we hope to give him to the zoo.

We resumed the journey to Kano. The bloody driver of the jeep was driving too fast and knocked down a camel which fortunately got up and hobbled away.

MONDAY 21 NOVEMBER

1966

Kano [*Nigeria*]

We arrived at Kano at 9am. Hot, dry, very crowded, open gutters on each side of the street, Agama lizards everywhere, females grey with yellow on head, males bright red head, red and blue tail. Small head frills. Scales very rough. They were on every wall and unbelievably fast. There were no flies in Kano. The begging is terrible, all the time, all the people.

We stopped at the Paradise hotel, ten and six a night, filthy bath and bog. Horace slept in the corner of the room, which became very hot and extremely smelly. De-ticked Horace and gave him a shampoo. Left him to dry on my bed but he crapped and it ran right through to the mattress. Mick chewed lettuce while I held his beak open.

THURSDAY 24 NOVEMBER
1966

Dear Mum and Dad,

We're pottering around in Ghana for a bit, and then we hope to get a job for about three months and get the boat back home (for about £49 on a passenger boat, third class, it might be cheaper on a cargo boat if we can find one). On the Sahara crossing Mick and I did nothing but talk about what we were going to eat when we get home: fishcakes, rissoles, fish and chips, chicken, shepherd's pie, bubble and squeak and a vast Chinese meal. Out here we eat bread and tinned sardines or corned beef, cooked yam, lots of oranges and endless banana sandwiches. We sold Horace yesterday to a children's school (they could only afford thirty shillings but as it's a good home we didn't mind). I would have liked to bring him home but I don't think we could ever have house-trained him and the export licence for animals is pretty steep.

FRIDAY 17 FEBRUARY

1967

The guy who gave us a lift in his jeep ran into a buzzard which we thought was dead so we stuck it in the back with us to eat later but alarmingly it suddenly woke up and, with a large sharp beak, started taking lumps out of everything within reach so we let it go.

We arrived in Algiers and went back to the hostel to discover that the toilet still hadn't been cleaned. The next morning we booked up to go steerage in the hold for £7 each on the boat to Marseilles. I went back to the botanical gardens and collected some of the painted frogs to take home. They were still the same specimens in the same gullies that we'd seen in November. The boat left at seven in the evening and took twenty-three hours to cross in terrible seas that seemed to be rising and falling so violently that we had to lie flat to stop being seasick. We were in the prow of the boat which was very crowded with Algerians who had had too much drink.

From Marseilles we got the train to London via Paris for 166 francs, which left us with just 20 francs in total. Northern France was ice-bound, and the Channel was cold and beautiful and I felt quite emotional as the cliffs of Dover came into view.

Julie's birthday. Gave her present.
Mummy ill so I stayed at
home to help. swept, tidied e
washed up e them ma
decided that she was all right
and I had to go to school.
Latin, french, English, art "
geography, scripture, maths, worn
out at end of day. lots of prep
Hemmed a thing on my sleeve
for needlework.
    Horrid day.

ANNEKA RICE

Anneka Rice is a broadcaster on television and radio. After her BBC training she worked as a journalist in Hong Kong and then shot to fame as the Skyrunner on Channel 4's Treasure Hunt. *She went on to devise the hit show* Challenge Anneka *in which she took on seemingly impossible tasks entirely with the help of donations and volunteers. Rice now works primarily as a Radio 2 DJ, dabbles in TV and is a keen artist.*

I've invented a new literary genre; part domestic manual, part thriller. My teenage years were turbulent to say the least. My sister Juliet, my one joyful constant, was born when I was 11. My mother, a brilliant woman born in the wrong generation, spent my teenage years breaking free from domesticity and reinventing herself. I was therefore left to juggle childcare with schoolwork and Saturday jobs; I cooked, wrote and sewed obsessively. Barely a day went by without a nursery drop off, a zip going in. I was young for my year – doing some of my O levels at 14. Half the time I wished I was just in a playground playing horses, instead of having to scale up to talk about boyfriends and smoking, even crowdfund a friend's abortion. Our house was party central. All this juxtaposed with looking after my sister, singing in the church choir and doing the ironing. My future role on *Challenge Anneka* was honed at a young age as I was the go-to person, the ultimate multitasker. The diaries are a rich source of social history, how teenagers in the 1970s could be left entirely to their own devices. Aged 16, I arrived in Paris for a French exchange, to be greeted not by the young girl and her family, but by a lone Frenchman. My boyfriend dramatically came to my rescue and we escaped to the south of France. Interpol wasn't scrambled. We had a nice holiday. No one ever knew. Or asked.

MONDAY 15 NOVEMBER 1971

Anneka is 13.

Juliet's 2nd birthday. Gave her present. Mummy ill, so I stayed at home to help. Swept, tidied and washed up and then Ma decided that she was alright and I had to go to school. Latin, French, English, Art, Geography, Scripture, Maths. Worn out at end of day. Lots of prep. Hemmed a thing on my sleeve for needlework. Horrid day.

WEDNESDAY 15 DECEMBER 1971

Juliet crying, I had to get up and help. Typical holidays. Got up, made bed, washed up, cleared up, looked after baby, unpicked hem of my skirt, hoovered all upstairs, tidied bedroom, tidied playroom. Mum said 'now you know what I do every day'.

SATURDAY 25 DECEMBER 1971

New Tape recorder. Taped *Pick of the Pops*. DJ annoying, talking over all the songs. I taped Juliet singing in the bath.

WEDNESDAY 5 JANUARY
1972

Tape recording at home. Julie useful for keeping her fingers on play and record while I do the sound effects and voices. Read *TV Producing and Script Writing* book.

TUESDAY 4 APRIL
1972

Superb day. Glen is lovely. Iona, Chris, Sue, Glen and I played tennis.

Waited for Glen to ring all evening. He did and we talked for ages. I rang him again at 9.15 and spoke till 10. Felt happy.

THURSDAY 27 APRIL
1972

In Guides we learned about childbirth and what to do as a mid-wife.

SATURDAY 29 APRIL
1972

Glen and Ant rang to say they could come to *Love Story* in the pm. It was fantastic and even better seeing it with Glen. Wrote to Glen in the evening.

SATURDAY 6 MAY

1972

Bought Nilsson 'Without You' for Glen in the morning.

SATURDAY 9 JUNE

1972

Black day. I went round to Rachel's in the evening. To my horror, Glen was there, with his arm round *Claire*. They left saying they had to go, but instead they just went round to the fire escape to Rachel's room. I didn't know this but went upstairs to see Ant; and there they were. I just said 'hello' brightly and stumbled down again. Tried to make a phone call but was crying so much I couldn't get the 2p in. Had to walk home in the rain. Taped some music but went over 'Killing Me Softly' by mistake and it finished me off.

FRIDAY 9 MARCH

1973

Rachel called round with Karen, then on to Frank's, and Ros came round, then Karen and Mong came, and then Jim came and then Dago with Ros, then Mong and Flea went and Snuff called round, then Karen and Dago went and me and Jim were left, then Dago and Mong and Flea came back and we stayed like that for 20 minutes.

TUESDAY 5 JUNE

1973

English Language O level. Chose 'In some animal
communities and in some human societies the female
dominates the male. Would it be a good thing if this came to
be the way of our society?' I just wrote 'Yes'. Then I crossed
it out but still said it's an obvious comment. Struggled to fill
two pages. In my world all the girls are in charge. Hope the
examiner is a woman.

MONDAY 8 OCTOBER

1973

In biology talked about contraception and Fi asked what sex
was like. Mrs Tennant said 'it's a very pleasant experience'. We
all went silent and pale with disgust. I will never be able to get
the picture out of my head. We didn't even laugh. We just felt
sick. Vol-au-vents for supper. Had a strange dream about Jerry.

TUESDAY 13 FEBRUARY

1973

Boring day. Got B for English and A- for history. We all tried to
get out of games. Fi drew a bruise on her ankle with mascara,
Foky put a bandage round her ankle, Clucky and Libby
weren't well. I tried to say I had a bad knee but the teacher
told me to go to surgery so I didn't go as she might have sent
me to hospital for an X-ray. In the end I had to play lacrosse

for one lesson and then I just went inside. Fanny's stitching went berserk in needlework.

SATURDAY 17 FEBRUARY
1973

Went to Croydon with Flea. Bought a pattern and a bra. Knocked masses of people about while carrying the huge roll of material to the counter. Had to lie on the floor I was laughing so much.

MONDAY 25 FEBRUARY
1974

Sue and I practised throwing a fag up and catching it in our mouths like Paul Newman. I got quite expert at it.

WEDNESDAY 8 MAY
1974

Disastrous day. Got told off by staff for bad behaviour. Explained I was exhausted by childcare duties on top of everything else.

WEDNESDAY 27 NOVEMBER
1974

Worst day ever. We have no money.

TUESDAY 9 DECEMBER

1974

Shown a film on Oxford Uni. No way I am going to be able to go to university. Need to start working. Wrote a letter to the BBC training department. Said I was 18.

TUESDAY 7 JANUARY

1975

Got a job at the record shop. Went in to learn the ropes.

SATURDAY 11 JANUARY

1975

Really enjoyed work. Graham [*Anneka's boss*] and I got on really well. I got at him all day about everywhere being in such a mess. Set up new system to file the records. Only got £2.50 but he said I'd get £3 next week. Was sorry when the day came to an end, it was so enjoyable.

FRIDAY 7 FEBRUARY

1975

Miss Ruhl said I would probably get an A for my A level French. She went on about Oxbridge. I didn't like to tell her I needed to leave school and get a job.

FRIDAY 18 JULY
1975

The French Exchange. Felt upset saying goodbye to Juliet and John [*John is Anneka's boyfriend at this point*], cried my heart out in the train. Made friends with Sophie and Philippe. We all went to have coffee in Paris when we arrived after 11 hours. Monsieur Heller was v nice but he was on his own as his wife and daughters were in Biarritz, so it was rather embarrassing and I didn't like to disturb him. He went out and left me with a key. Had a look at the Eiffel T and it was vast. Men kept trying to chat me up so I ran back and couldn't open the door. Concierge had to do it.

SUNDAY 20 JULY
1975

Went on the metro to Le Louvre ... Horrid blokes wouldn't leave me alone. A bloke asked if he could walk with me and I felt in need of company and as he seemed polite I said yes. He asked if he could possibly take me out cos the moment he saw me he thought it'd be something special. I ran off. Locked out again.

THURSDAY 24 JULY
1975

Panicking cos of money I am having to spend. Meal cost £2.50, only have £10 for whole trip.

FRIDAY 25 JULY

1975

Ordered a coffee; it was 60p. Felt so upset because I'd just cashed an English pound and it practically all went on that. Desperately homesick.

SUNDAY 27 JULY

1975

V upset all morning and couldn't stop crying. I rang John and he said he'd rescue me.

THURSDAY 31 JULY

1975

John picked me up at 7am in the Alfa Romeo. I yelled 'au revoir' up the stairs and off I went. Mr Heller watching anxiously from a window. I waved. And then opened the windows and screamed with joy.

THURSDAY 25 MARCH

1976

Interview with the BBC. Didn't tell anyone, got train to London. The lady was v. friendly and I pretended I had lots of journalistic experience. It was so exciting walking through the BBC door. I will get paid to do the course, if I get it. Even if I end up making coffee and typing scripts at least I'll be typing interesting things. I'll do anything just to have somewhere to go next term.

TUESDAY 28 SEPTEMBER
1976

Really nice people on the course. John is nice and Cathy. We have to write an insert for *Woman's Hour*.

MONDAY 13 DECEMBER
1976

Today we find out our postings. I get the World Service at Bush House. I don't even know what this is. Exciting. Apparently I'll be in a studio with a stopwatch in my hand within half an hour.

23 Monday Thought John Week 26 was dead today. Needless to say he wasn't : PHEW! Wrote some letters still raining yeuch! Had bad day at school, wore both my cool new jumpers! ate and drank too much.

24 Tuesday Posted letters, Princess Margaret landed at school in her helicopter. Got 95% in maths went to meeting about the trip to america. I have NOT washed my hair. I am very very Tired.

25 Wednesday Ill off school today with Diarrhea. Went Swimming in High Wycombe with Nan and Grandad Jumped off the high board a few times. Learnt the goliwoux solution. Blew up my Dinghy. lads tip for the world cup (france) are out.

26 Thursday Had my Piano lesson. Went to Mat (K)s for the evening. Rode his pony Dreamer' for a while which was fun. Had Lasagne. Climbed a big tree. Watched Eastenders Streaming Hayfever - Pollen count 83 - Had a nice cold bath

ROB DEERING

*Rob Deering is a stand-up comedian,
musician, writer and avid marathon runner.
He was born in London in 1972.*

Surely the 1980s was the most excruciating decade to be
a teenager? Imagine feeling crushingly uncool at a time
when even the coolest superstars were self-conscious,
preposterously dressed and deeply ill-at-ease. The internet
has empowered cynicism and studied irony – along with
giving everyone the comfort of knowing that whatever social
faux pas they might make, there will ALWAYS be someone
sadder on Facebook; but in my day, if you were the biggest
idiot at school, you were the biggest idiot IN THE WORLD.

In 1985 I hung around with a pretty cool group of old-
before-our-time rebels in London. Some of them were girls!
In 1987 I discovered how much I like standing up in front of
people and making them laugh – and they liked it too!

But I only kept a diary in 1986, assiduously recording
the year when I moved to the country, and social oblivion;
where my directionless-but-effortful quest to look – and be –

different did not meet with even the low levels of approval it had in the city. My diary records a year of big meals, bad clothes, and lots and lots of TV. I'm sad in it, frankly, but hey, if you can't go a little off-piste in the quest-for-the-self when you're 13, when can you? I was Adrian Mole incarnate, and I'm not ashamed.

(I'm a bit ashamed.)

TUESDAY 7 JANUARY

1986

Rob is 13.

Snowed like (wow) chronic dandruff!! Saw *You Only Live Twice* on the Gogglebox.

WEDNESDAY 8 JANUARY

1986

Wet and horrible out, but the lasagne I had was lovely.

SATURDAY 11 JANUARY

1986

Had excellent dream about flying gas. There was a good film on TV about a robbery.

SUNDAY 12 JANUARY

1986

John took us to Pizza Hut (wow).

SATURDAY 18 JANUARY

1986

Had *superb* lasagne and stayed up late alone. (Fun, eh?)

SUNDAY 19 JANUARY

1986

Went to a fantastic rope swing at Chanctonbury Ring (cool).

MONDAY 27 JANUARY

1986

Sent home for 70% of the day. *Daisy Pulls It Off* finishes Feb. 15th.

TUESDAY 28 JANUARY

1986

Seeing *Daisy* on Saturday.

WEDNESDAY 29 JANUARY

1986

Got tickets for *Daisy* – only £6!!! Saw prospective new school – looks good.

THURSDAY 30 JANUARY
1986

Had lasagne, watched *Treasure Hunt*.

SATURDAY 1 FEBRUARY
1986

ONE OF THE BEST DAYS EVER!! SAW *DAISY PULLS IT OFF* AGAIN WITH RICH AND BEX. THE WOMAN WHO PLAYED MONICA TOOK OUR PROGRAMMES TO BE AUTOGRAPHED BY THE WHOLE CAST! AFTER THE (BRILLIANT) SHOW I WENT BACKSTAGE TO GET THE PROGRAMMES AND MET DAISY AND TRIXIE!!! ALSO GOT HIGHEST SCORE YET ON COMMANDO.

SUNDAY 2 FEBRUARY
1986

Headachey, stunned and overwhelmed after yesterday.

WEDNESDAY 5 FEBRUARY
1986

It's snowing!!! Was sent home, and walked a long, long way. Oh! *DAISY PULLS IT OFF*, sigh.

THURSDAY 6 FEBRUARY

1986

Thick snow. I hope I can do some sledging. Went to a new drama club.

FRIDAY 7 FEBRUARY

1986

Got sent home so I went sledging!!! (GOOD, EH!) OH, DAISY DAISY DAISY, sigh.

THURSDAY 13 FEBRUARY

1986

Drama club was great, and Thursday is the best TV evening of the week.

MONDAY 17 FEBRUARY

1986

At Nan's. Mum had op tonight. Saw *Spies Like Us*, which was brilliant.

THURSDAY 20 FEBRUARY
1986

A busy day: visited Mum, saw *Brewster's Millions* (which was good), had a Pizza Hut, went to drama and saw Mum again. Back home tonight.

MONDAY 24 FEBRUARY
1986

Mum is home from the hospital and I am back at school. Matthew bought me a yo-yo on Friday which I love.

FRIDAY 28 FEBRUARY
1986

We move today. We are here. I have phoned a few people and have flown a kite.

SATURDAY 1 MARCH
1986

PACKED SOME WARDROBES, CHECKED OUT LOFT. Had early evening doze.

MONDAY 3 MARCH

1986

First day of school and the last if it doesn't improve. I am very tired.

THURSDAY 6 MARCH

1986

Got new desk, desk chair, table and table/trolley. They are ultra – man. Have changed rooms so that mine can be redecorated.

FRIDAY 7 MARCH

1986

Went to see our next-door-neighbours who are very nice. My room is now WHITE.

MONDAY 17 MARCH

1986

Got punched by fucking wanker 3rd year. Got superb lamp for room. Oh Gabrielle, Gabrielle.

TUESDAY 18 MARCH

1986

Keep getting hiccups and tummy aches. Chair for room is coming tomorrow! Lasagne for tea this evening.

THURSDAY 20 MARCH

1986

End of term today. Not feeling well, and sick of this hellhole. AND I have to wake up tomorrow at 9.00. FUCKING HELL.

FRIDAY 21 MARCH

1986

Got superb bed and won a dairy hamper in a raffle. Still have a bad cold.

MONDAY 7 APRIL

1986

It's freezing outside. Back to stupid school, without any dinner money I went. Began to sort out a box of stuff.

TUESDAY 8 APRIL
1986

Had dinner money today. Finished the box and cooked tea for me and Dad in my room.

WEDNESDAY 9 APRIL
1986

My room is now almost perfect. All my pictures, posters and new curtains *COOL*. I have also a new alarm clock.

FRIDAY 11 APRIL
1986

Nan & Grandad are staying tonight. Have stuck a selection of pictures from Paris on my wall. My palm tree slippers are cool.

WEDNESDAY 16 APRIL
1986

Cooked shepherd's pie on cooker. Have tidied my desk and made it so ultra cool you might die!!

MONDAY 21 APRIL
1986

Got up as normal and went in the loo. It was a long time before I came out and I was off school with diarrhoea all day.

TUESDAY 6 MAY
1986

If there is a God I hate him and it is mutual. Ill yet again today. It had to be Tuesday. Have started reading *Absolute Beginners*, which John gave me.

MONDAY 12 MAY
1986

My camera has arrived and it is fantastic! It does everything, wind-on, the lot!

TUESDAY 13 MAY
1986

Took some photos, went to the Red Lion for an immense tea. Mucked about coolwise on a synth at lunchtime. Am missing all my friends.

MONDAY 19 MAY

1986

Got haircut, model plane, Action Man rope launcher and an Aerobie. An Aerobie is a ring which flies long distances. Me and Scott played with it in his field.

TUESDAY 20 MAY

1986

My hair is brilliant! It was wet and rainy all day, but I got a good go on the Aerobie with Jonathan. I have got a new cap. Nan and Grandad are staying. Don't think that I've forgotten Gabrielle!!

MONDAY 23 JUNE

1986

Thought John was dead today. Needless to say, he wasn't. *PHEW* Had bad day at school. Wore both my cool new jumpers!

TUESDAY 24 JUNE

1986

Princess Margaret landed at school in her helicopter. Got 95% in Maths. Went to meeting about the trip to America. I have NOT washed my hair. I am very very tired.

in support of those who were gonna be made redundant. Arthur Scargill won't hold a National Ballot to see if the majority of GB's miners want to strike. Now only Nottinghamshire's miners are still going to work & pickets are trying to stop them.

British Airways, which will be privatised next year, suggest its the most profitable airline in the world!! It made a profit of £181 million (<u>more than</u> 1.3 times great than last year). Britain's industry is booming now too!

Well, I'm working hard. I had a Latin test today, on Virgil Aeneid VI & I think I did O.K - actually quite well.

Today's Mayday. In Russia they had their annual May Day Parade in Red Square. The new Leader (only 3 months in office) Chernenko seems well established now.

Well I guess I'll go to sleep now. Good night & sweet dreams.

May 2nd Wed. 09.15 pm Dear Philip,

I'm watching "Entertainment USA" - it's in Puerto Rico today. I watched more of the "Sound of Music" today. Haven't got much to write. Mum & Dad were rowing this morning again I think 'cos Mum's been crying a lot. I don't think I'm getting enough revision done so goodbye "A" grades on my O'levels. Well, good night.

May 5th Sat. 12.27 pm Dear Philip,

I'm doing prep. at my desk. Mohan Uncle & everyone from Bombay came yesterday & they're great. The 2 kids, Rishub (Male) & Ritika (female) are so sweet & good. They've almost all gone + Sheena & Salim to Oxford St.

SAMIRA AHMED

Samira Ahmed was born in 1968 and grew up in south London. After studying at Oxford, she became a BBC news trainee, and worked on Newsnight *and the* Today *programme. She joined* Channel 4 News *in 2000, and is now a freelance journalist and presenter of Radio 4's arts programme* Front Row.

I've kept a diary since I was 11. I still love choosing the next notebook, but the 1985 Athena cocktail cover was my favourite. It reminds me of how much I balanced exams with pop music, frosted make-up and books and fantasy films. I turned 16 in 1984 and these years were full of my yearning for the escape to university. I love that as a studious, geeky schoolgirl I had beautiful handwriting. Except when I was cross.

All my diaries still live in a pile in a cupboard but I hadn't re-read them since I wrote them, so had no inkling of how emotionally unsettling it would be. The first few days of turning the pages I was transported back as if in a psychological time machine to years of forgotten anguish.

But then I realised how much joy was in there too, and spotted all these connections I'd never noticed, which revealed my character and my journalistic ambition: like my detailed note-taking on who shot Bobby Ewing in *Dallas*, my obsession with news and with learning to drive, and my shock at being stitched up as an exchange student by a German newspaper.

The accounts of my dreams remind me of the underlying mental anxiety 1980s Cold War teenagers carried in our daily lives. I can't believe how many nightmares I had about nuclear annihilation alongside the sweet dreams about David Bowie. I still think I could have shared my Mr Spock dream. But my husband says best not.

TUESDAY 1 MAY

1984

Samira is 15.

Watching the News. Several guns and weapons have been found in the Libyan embassy, and the suspected murderers of WPC Fletcher have been narrowed down to two, both diplomats, and therefore not allowed to be prosecuted. They're all free. The PM talks of it as a 'national humiliation' for us and it is.

The coal miners' dispute is still going on. Arthur Scargill won't hold a National ballot to see if the majority of GB's miners want to strike.

British Airways, which will be privatised next year, says it's the most profitable airline in the world!! It made a profit of 181 million pounds. Britain's industry is booming now too!

TUESDAY 22 MAY

1984

I've just watched *Dallas* and it was really good/bad. I mean good in the sense that Barnes has at last hit oil, but I only hope that he hasn't already committed suicide or worse – i.e. shot Bobby. You see – someone intended to shoot JR, but shot Bobby by accident. It could be:

a/ Cliff Barnes b/ Von (JR's crooked lawyer/banker) c/ Sue Ellen d/ Edgar Randolph (who was blackmailed earlier in series) e/ Peter Richards f/ Katherine Wentworth or even g/ Clayton Farlow or h/ JR himself or even i/ Pam (doubtful).

We taped it and noticed the reflection of a man with dark hair in a door as the murderer went in so we can narrow it down to 3 possibilities. Cliff Barnes, Edgar Randolph and JR. That's just my deductions, though.

Tomorrow on *Breakfast Time* on TV there's going to be a phone-in and discussion about who shot Bobby Ewing. The thing was, everyone suspected that JR was going to be shot so it was no surprise that *someone* was. But when Bobby Ewing (poor, sweet, loving harmless Bobby!!) fell out of JR's chair with blood on his forehead, I was really totally stunned and shocked. That was the last thing I expected! Well, I guess everyone at school will be talking about it tomorrow.

WEDNESDAY 20 JULY

1984

Woke up at 09.50. I was the last one to wake up (as usual)!

We took the train to Northwick Park. After lunch we went to Brent Cross Shopping Centre – what an amazing place! Abbas Uncle picked us up at 7.30 and we went back to Shaheen's place – us girls went upstairs and practised our Gharba dance. We had dinner out in the garden and then danced to music, teaching each other steps and trying on Shaheen's straw hat.

FRIDAY 22 JULY

1984

As we had nothing to do we stayed at home all day putting mehndi [*Indian henna tattoos*] on our left hands using toothpicks while we watched a Jerry Lewis film. Then we went to Shaheen's house for dinner. Hamid and Aiyla were also there and Seema Auntie. For dinner we had a delicious chicken tikka thing, baigan ka bharta, (spicy) naan, red cabbage and carrot salad, cucumber and coke to drink. For dessert there was caramel pudding!

We read this awful book by some fanatic about what he thought to be rights and wrongs in the eyes of Islam. What a MALE CHAUVINIST PIG!!!!

There was also a ghazzal party of sorts, and all us girls had to sing songs from Bollywood films. We left to go home at about 2.15am.

P.S. Katherine Wentworth shot Bobby – and on purpose too.

SATURDAY 8 FEBRUARY

1986

I had my first driving lesson with Luke – he's a really nice, totally ordinary, instructor and I drove up and down the High Street for ages.

WEDNESDAY 12 FEBRUARY

1986

It was Dad's birthday today. Mum made a lovely cake with a single candle which we took into his room at 7.45am. He's begun growing a moustache. He just told me that within two years the Westland helicopter company, which has just been taken over by the Americans, will be in serious trouble. As he requested, I make a note of this for posterity.

FRIDAY 14 FEBRUARY

1986

3 point turns in my driving lesson yesterday. Luke said he considers me in his top 25% of pupils. I need to get higher.

WEDNESDAY 19 MARCH

1986

I went for a driving lesson. I am now officially in Luke's top 3 best pupils.

TUESDAY 25 MARCH

1986

Today I finished what turned out to be a six-side essay on *The Mill on the Floss*. Had a driving lesson in which my instructor told me that I was the best of his pupils and got me to drive this other girl so she could see how bad she was in comparison.

TUESDAY 15 APRIL

1986

I felt deeply morbid and ominous because of the U.S. military bombing of Libya last night using troops and planes stationed here in Britain.

For Monday we have to prepare to speak our opinions in German on the American bombing of Libya and Colonel Gaddafi. I jokingly commented that the world may have been bombed out of existence by Monday.

If the bomb drops I want to be right under it.

WEDNESDAY 23 APRIL

1986

I had a two-hour driving lesson and my instructor was very pleased with the way I managed my reversing round a corner up a hill.

THURSDAY 8 MAY

1986

I passed my driving test for the first time this morning.

MONDAY 12 MAY
1986

On Friday night I dreamed of David Bowie. He loved me and I had to escape down Oxford Street and wandered into a huge banqueting hall where an Indian wedding reception was going on. I walked out, and met David Bowie again outside a shop with a postcard stand. He held my hand and didn't let go.

MONDAY 28 MAY
1986

On Saturday night I dreamed of nuclear war – floods, killer Triffid-type plants and being killed by the explosion of a nuclear power plant. And even as I threw myself down on the ground I thought, thank God, at least I'm going to die right away, no lingering. Yes I must be close enough to just melt. And I hadn't even touched the ground when the explosion came.

THURSDAY 15 MAY
1986

My German oral actually went very well. I chatted about: Ronald Reagan and politics; my parents and how they came here, the status of Indian women in society, and Oxford and my future. Mrs James and I laughed so much during our chat, and afterwards she asked me where in Oxford I was going to, because she has a friend in her second year at St Peter's reading Geography.

WEDNESDAY 11 JUNE

1986

One very frightening effect of exams is the way they make you shut yourself off from the world's events. I haven't been able to touch a newspaper or watch the TV bulletins for days. Watching the 5.45pm news today and reading the *Guardian* was like water to a man dying of thirst – I was so eager for all the information I had missed I could hardly slow my mind down to read and listen and take everything in.

SUNDAY 15 JUNE

1986

[*Birthday.*] Eighteen. I feel so unaffected. It's a lovely hot summer's day like yesterday and forecasts say it'll last at least to the end of June. I got up at 8 and had a bath, and then went into Mum's room where they all gave me my presents. I got a black leather briefcase and a lovely watch from Mum and Dad. Sheru gave me some lavender bags, the Housemartins' single 'Happy Hour', and two books. We cut the cake there too. It was lovely.

I can't imagine myself going out into the big world and meeting new people and enjoying myself. I can see me staying at home, reading, watching TV and going out now and then with Sheru, but for anything more, well, I've just got so sheltered and introverted. I feel a little strange that I'm on the threshold of freedom. I feel that's it's all going to waste. I should be out there, living life and having wonderful new experiences.

New Year Resolutions for 1969:
  I resolve to :-
Be happy and make others happy
Not maul the dog.
Be kind and thoughtful.
Not watch too much television.
Read a lot of good books.
Not to eat too much or
between meals
leave my nails <u>alone</u>.

This flower came
by Air Mail from
Autie Betty in
Spain.

JANET ELLIS

Janet Ellis MBE *was born in Kent in 1955. She began presenting* Jigsaw *in 1979, at the age of 24, and in 1983 got a job on flagship children's show* Blue Peter, *which she fronted until 1987. Now an author, her first novel,* The Butcher's Hook, *was published in 2016.*

If I'd never kept a diary, I'm sure I would have conveniently forgotten what I was like as a young teenager. I might have remembered the passions – to be an actress, to get on okay at school, to have friends – but I could gloss over any meanness, trivial behaviour and childish obsessions. To meet myself in embryo is both appalling and wonderful. I can't deny that my waistline/boys/getting wolf-whistled mattered then, there's actual proof in my own handwriting, but I'm comforted those things went alongside hours making doll's clothes, hanging out with my mother and trying to eat the white of a soft-boiled egg without gagging. I'm glad I mention reading good books; I love the quick, almost 'of course' reference to *Blue Peter*; I can see I genuinely loved my family and my home. I'm embarrassed by my rush to judgements, my desperation to meet boys and, OH MY GOD, MY MOTHER SHAVED UNDER MY ARMS.

It's a privilege to reach back over the years and tell little Miss Ellis that she did become an actress, her weight will cease to be an issue and at least three of those New Year resolutions are worth sticking to. What she might say to me is less clear, but I think she'd probably have been a tad disappointed by how often I maul the dog. Soft-boiled egg white is still off the menu, by the way.

WEDNESDAY 1 JANUARY

1969

Janet is 13.

Ring out the old, ring in the new. Ring out the false, ring in the true!

Last night I stayed up till 11 o'clock watching a super film about breaking the sound barrier and Ma got me up at 12 to welcome in the New Year. I had a glass of Dubonnet.

New Year's Resolutions for 1969. I resolve to:

Be happy and make others happy
Not maul the dog
Be kind and thoughtful
Not watch too much television
Read a lot of good books
Not to eat too much or in between meals
Leave my nails alone

SATURDAY 4 JANUARY

1969

Today has been ever so exciting – first of all the post delivered my audition results – I'VE PASSED! I've DONE it, I am AN ACTRESS! I'm so proud now, we phoned all the relatives up to tell them – I'm so pleased! The uniform list is huge and it isn't quite definite I'll go there – we're applying for a council grant. The thing is, the fees are £90 per term and the journey up there is by bus, tube and train which is strenuous. Tap dancing is also done there – lovely.

SUNDAY 5 JANUARY

1969

Still cannot get over passing audition – head TWICE the usual size!

Auntie Betty gave me a present – a gorgeous, gorgeous nightdress case – never, ever have I seen nicer – in form of a doll.

MONDAY 6 JANUARY

1969

Today I stuffed rags into the nightie case Auntie Betty gave, and I am going to use her for a doll ornament on my bed – she is super! I think she is far too good to haul a nightie in and out of!

Made another puppet doll, about 9" high, operated by placing 2 fingers inside the body, hand hidden by the skirt.

On a self-imposed food cut down – one sweet per day, etc.

TUESDAY 7 JANUARY

1969

Today I began sewing a complete winter wardrobe for Sharon's doll.

Have also started making furniture for Victorian dolls house – a job more difficult than I thought.

FRIDAY 17 JANUARY
1969

Had brekkies in dressing gown today which was lovely. Then got dressed and went to the dentist. I went in first and the man froze up half my face with a sweet-tasting spray. Awful. Then he gave me four fillings, all drilled unbearably on the nerve. The one he froze me up for hurt despite it. One made me retch because it was to the side and uncomfortable. Now have 19 fillings.

TUESDAY 21 JANUARY
1969

Hope to hear from Kent Educational Committee SOON! Am desperate to know whether or not I will go to school or not. Hope violently I do!! In science tasted some distilled water – it was sort of flat and smelt like peppermint.

MONDAY 27 JANUARY
1969

Today in elocution I practised vowels and resonance and the usual breathing. For vowels we did monophthongs, diphthongs and triphthongs. I'm still not sure of what they mean or if the spellings are right. In drama club, we did feeling through our bodies (like getting into a cold shower on a hot day) which was fun and I do wish people wouldn't muck about. After the lesson we told Jo that we were having trouble with the grant and she said, it didn't matter, cos I had a lot of talent. PHEW! I'm so pleased she thinks I'm good. When I hear things like that I walk on air – I'm even more determined to ACT – as if I'd ever do ANYTHING else!! Sometimes I think that drama flows in my veins instead of blood!

SUNDAY 23 FEBRUARY
1969

Today Ma measured me – me vital statistics! – and I am 32–25-33 which is pretty silly! I am on a campaign (not another, said Ma). I'm going to lose 3" off my waistline in 2 weeks – 1½" per week – aaaaah! It means cutting down on cakes, sweets, potatoes etc. and all the other horrid things I have to give up – still everyone suffers to look beautiful, which is what I remind myself as I break the teeth of my comb dragging it through my tangled locks!

TUESDAY 4 MARCH
1969

Freezing cold again, and Ma and Pa went out house hunting and found two houses they like. Both are in the Greater

London area which is out of question for Arts Educational School – we have been turned down by them now. I'm not going to the school. Am very, very, very, very, very, very, very, very, very, very sad.

FRIDAY 7 MARCH
1969

When I came home today there was no one here. Ma and Pa arrived about 1½ hours after, and they'd made an offer on a house in St Margaret's near Richmond. About an hour after that, the estate agent phoned to say our offer had been accepted and now we have a house (almost!). It is near the skating rink, and 5 minutes from shops and river. It has 4 bedrooms. I'm going to see it on Sunday. All this is very exciting but in some ways I'll be sorry to leave.

SUNDAY 9 MARCH
1969

Today we went to see 14, St Margaret's Drive, St Margaret's – the house we are having (touch wood!). I saw it for the first time and I must say I loved it!! It has a lovely bright orange front door – in fact, practically the whole house is bright orange or yellow – the owner's favourite colour.

WEDNESDAY 9 APRIL

1969

Today the weather was hot and Ma lent me a skirt – well, she's given it to me, actually. Anyhow, I wanted to wear a short-sleeved blouse with it but my family have been telling me I am practically Swedish in my charmpits, and Ma said she'd shave me. So it was done. A momentous day, I shaved for the first time! (Or rather, Ma shaved me!)

THURSDAY 24 APRIL

1969

Played dolls with Sharon [*Janet's sister*] and made a wig for mine as her hair is a bit sparse! Rather wet weather – what the weather-man would call a 'low depression'! Watched *Blue Peter* as per usual.

THURSDAY 1 MAY

1969

Today I made a wee house in a wooden box. I used cardboard to make teeny chairs, tables, chest of drawers, pianos (yes, I really did make a piano!). I made wee sofas, chairs, and carpets. I embroidered felt pictures, and it still isn't finished. Tomorrow I mean to finish it.

THURSDAY 19 JUNE
1969

Ma came in to say we ought to get up and we did! Had breakfast (I ate nearly all of my soft-boiled WHITE of the egg and only retched twice) then we collected all our stuff up and left. Arrived at new house round 10.30 and waited for the removal men.

Went to the pub to get sandwiches (which were ghastly I thought), and ate them sitting on floor on packing cases.

FRIDAY 20 JUNE
1969

The lady next door has invited us all for drinks tomorrow, which is very nice. She has a 14-year-old son – but he took (and passed) French O level at 13 and is taking seven this year and Ma says he's probably 4' high and dull as ditchwater, but as I haven't SEEN him yet I'm crossing my fingers. Ma and Pa went to the shops today and put up the curtains and mine look LOVELY!

MONDAY 23 JUNE
1969

Today I had a bad attack of nerves – but I didn't cry or anything – just did piles of diarrhoea. We went up to my school very early. Ma plonked me on some people from my form, and they just giggled amongst themselves for ages. Anyhow, I've got a place to next to a girl called Dawn who wears glasses. There are several nice people in my class – but 99% of them are common … but they are still nice! Trouble is, they all (well, most of them) read silly love comics and giggle at nudes. I hope I do get to like this school.

TUESDAY 24 JUNE

1969

After games everyone takes a shower, and a lot of naked girls leap in and out saying 'ooh it's boiling' which is a change from 'ugh it's cold' – and nice to see they're not silly about everyone being nude! Just smile at everyone in sight and act natural and already I feel I've been there longer than a day!

THURSDAY 14 AUGUST

1969

This morning Ma got a tape measure and measured me – and now my waist is 24" – this is goody as it used to be 25"! My hips are 34" and my bust is 32" – if I could lose my stomach and put an extra 2" on my bust it would be super! Am holding my tummy in all the time, and can now pull it into a hollow!

THURSDAY 30 JULY

1970

Tomorrow Ma, Sharon and I are going into Richmond as I need a new bra and S needs some slacks. My bust is now 34" ('oh!' I hear you exclaim in some horror!!), S is 25" and Ma is 32". Ma said I get the size from Pa's side of the family, but I say it's all mine!

MONDAY 10 AUGUST

1970

I have grown and am now just over 5'3". Oh for 1 and a ½ or so more inches!

THURSDAY 13 AUGUST

1970

Today when I was walking to drama I got a total of *5* wolf whistles! To say nothing of innumerable glances, looks, and "'ello darlin'"s! Very morale boosting, I must say!

Our Lady's Saturday, s, *white.*

What a day!! We had a terrific time in Dublin. Everything seemed to go for us! We had terrific fun on the train going up & coming down, & Granny gave us a smashing dinner & tea. We had no trouble in getting buses, & we got a terrific view of the match. The final score was 9-9, & boy, was it some match!! I didn't get home until eleven.

If thou takest my part, O sweet Lady, what can harm me? Give me thy blessing, and say: I will act as mediatrix on thy behalf, and therefore fear not.

TERRY WOGAN

Legendary broadcaster Sir Terry Wogan was born in Ireland in 1938, the son of a grocer. His broadcasting career included the Radio 2 breakfast show, his own primetime chat show, and many years hosting the Eurovision Song Contest *and* Children in Need. *Sir Terry was knighted in 2005. He died in 2016.*

Harriet Jaine, producer of My Teenage Diary: Terry Wogan's 'Catholic Diary of 1953' was small, leather-bound and dog-eared. I was honoured when he entrusted me with it for a couple of weeks at the beginning of 2014. The diary's publishers had thoughtfully ended each page with a 'Bible quote for the day', and peppered the diary with reminders of religious holidays, fasts and reasons to go to church. Inside, the pages were filled with Wogan's neat schoolboy cursive, always written in blue fountain pen. His days were filled with trips to the cinema (he remembered spending the entire afternoon at the pictures, sometimes watching two films back to back), lazy Saturday mornings (3 January: 'Had our dinner in bed'), and long and involved Subbuteo tournaments between him and his friends (recorded in minute detail). Not much cast a shadow over this sunny existence, apart from the odd beating from a teacher, about which the adult Terry was characteristically gracious and forgiving. Never afraid to laugh at himself, Wogan was a charming and generous interviewee who was tickled by his obsession with table soccer and remembered his childhood with deep affection.

At the front of Terry's diary:
Terentius Wogan, Limericense, Hibernia

FRIDAY 2 JANUARY
1953

Terry is 14.

We went to town in the afternoon with Mammy. Brian bought a popgun. In the night we went to *Sinbad the Sailor*. It was the funniest panto I've been at this year.

SATURDAY 3 JANUARY
1953

Stayed in bed all morning. Had our dinner in bed. At about 3 o'clock in the afternoon we went up Dorset Street and bought stamps. Came home and then went with Auntie May to the Bohemian near Dalymount Park. Main picture was good, but the shorts were bad.

SUNDAY 4 JANUARY
1953

Went to 11.30 Mass. In the afternoon, we went with Auntie Kitty to the Green cinema. Saw two good pictures, *Boots Malone* and *Storm over Tibet*. I stayed in all night.

MONDAY 5 JANUARY

1953

Brian and I stayed in bed all morning. At 5 o'clock in the afternoon the taxi came. We got a good seat in the train and arrived in Limerick at 9.10. James called over in the night. I got the shock of my life when I found I had got 6th place in the class.

Bible quote of the day: 'Meditation is to prayer what study is to wisdom.'

TUESDAY 6 JANUARY

1953

After Mass I went down to Sextons and Billy, James and I made arrangements for the Table Soccer League. We then went for a walk. In the night I played Table Soccer.

WEDNESDAY 7 JANUARY

1953

I stayed in bed all morning and then Billy called. In the afternoon I played the Table Soccer League with J. Horgan. I beat him 6–3. Billy wasn't able to play his match with James, so after tea James and I had a friendly.

THURSDAY 8 JANUARY
1953

In the afternoon I beat Horgan 9–2. In the night I refereed the match between James and Billy. It was a draw 4–4. I stayed on at Billy's house until 10.30.

FRIDAY 9 JANUARY
1953

In the morning I played my soccer match with James. I was beaten by James 5–1. I played terrible. In the afternoon I went to *Don't Bother to Knock*. It was an atrocious picture. *A Millionaire for Christy* made up for it though.

THURSDAY 15 JANUARY
1953

Went back to school today. Brian had a bad cold so he didn't go. In the afternoon went to Horgan's to watch the match between him and James. James won 12–4. Mammy went out during the night.

WEDNESDAY 21 JANUARY
1953

Mr Marmion threw out six boys for six slaps this morning.

The afternoon was uneventful and after school I went down to James's house to watch the match between John Sexton and Horgan. It was a terrific match. Horgan won 9–8. I got my postal order today so I will send away for the Vamping Chart and Ventrilo tomorrow.

FRIDAY 13 FEBRUARY
1953

Friar Durnin forgot to send me out today. Surprise of the week! Friar Macloughlin walked in and told us that we'd have a half day today because a lot of staff were down with flu. Looking forward to Rugby International in Dublin tomorrow.

SATURDAY 14 FEBRUARY
1953

What a day!! We had a terrific time in Dublin. Everything seemed to go for us! We had terrific fun on the train going up and coming down, and Granny gave us a smashing dinner and tea. We had no trouble in getting buses, and we got a terrific view of the match. The final score was 9–9 and boy, was it some match!! I didn't get home until eleven.

MONDAY 11 MAY
1953

Got kept in by Friar Durnin. Went to tennis courts afternoon and had a few games. After my ekkers [*'exercises', or homework*] were done I mowed the lawn.

TUESDAY 12 MAY
1953

Got six slaps and detention from Dirty Durnin. After detention went to Rosbrien and we won 3–1 after being led 1-nil at half time. I made the last goal.

MONDAY 3 AUGUST
1953

My birthday today! It was a blazing hot day but we couldn't go anywhere because of the Bank Holiday. Uncle Eddie and Auntie Diana came down for the day with Bill in their new car. I got £4 in cash and a camera.

MONDAY 10 AUGUST

1953

Served my first Mass today. I made a good few mistakes. At 11 o'clock James, Billy and I went on a picnic to the Clare Gardens. We had a terrific day.

TUESDAY 11 AUGUST

1953

Served second Mass this morning. No mistakes. After breakfast played tennis in the Country with James. 9–7, 3–6, 4–4. After dinner went to Dentist to have my tooth pulled. Ouch!??!

FRIDAY 18 DECEMBER

1953

Got our holidays today at 3.30pm. Mum told me that we were going to Dublin on Sunday, and that Uncle Charlie was bringing us up.

FRIDAY 25 DECEMBER

1953

Went to 11.30 Mass with Dad. After Mass we went for a walk. Fed my face at dinner and tea and read my books in between meals. Played Lotto and cards until 1.30.

SATURDAY 2 JANUARY

1953

Saw *Dick Whittington* in the Olympia with Cecil Sheridan. Extremely good. Cecil himself was a hoot. The best panto I've seen in a long time.

24 Monday

8 am

Leaving for holidays.

9

Rushed around all day doing things
in town. Picked up photos of Jocelyn
+ Ingrid.

11

Met Ingrid at the squat, then we
went out for a meal in W.
Kensington. ~~Wester two~~ Had good
talk with each other. I really like
Ingrid.

2

Then we went to the writers' group
— last one — in a while!

4

Got my new name — Oh!

5

AKANKE ÎFE

6

Diane brought along list.
Discussed "Reflections" Jocelyn Haight
Awore wasn't strong enuf. Said
a sad goodbye.

August

Sunday	2	9	16	23	30
Monday	3	10	17	24	**31**
Tuesday	4	11	18	25	
Wednesday	5	12	19	26	
Thursday	6	13	20	27	
Friday	7	14	21		
Saturday					

Notes

JACKIE KAY

Jackie Kay was born in Edinburgh in 1961. Her first book of poetry, The Adoption Papers, *was published in 1991, and deals with issues of identity, race and sexuality. Kay is the third modern Makar – Scotland's national poet.*

It is strange looking back on your teenage self. She is right there and yet she's far away. She reminds you of yourself. If I was to try and stop her to ask her to tell me a bit more about myself then, she'd probably say, 'Can't stop, got to go to a meeting.'

I hadn't properly remembered that I'd kept any diary entries. It was only looking back through old boxes that I came across these. And although they don't give much detail, they reminded me of the proximity of things.

That I could write in one entry about both fascist posters going up about me and getting an 'A' on Yeats for English tells me all I need to remember about my teenage self! A little later in the diary, there's an entry for a public meeting that we organised to counter the fascist posters (it tells you that

250 people attended eight days later). I remember speaking at that public meeting and quoting Angela Davis: 'If they come in the morning …' It seemed even more important to speak out after people had tried to silence you. It still does. And even though these entries make me cringe a little, I stand by my old teenage self. She made it through with the help of her friends. I remember when my black friends Mo and Olivette and Ingrid came to Stirling to visit. I had never felt so accompanied. That feeling has not left me. And writing too has become a lifelong companion.

22 AUGUST

1976

Jackie is 14.

Supremacist Syrup

Like a black child
Standing behind the fence
Of the playground
Watching white kids
Scream skid slide
Down shoots, sing on swings,
I watch you play

Oh, I know it's not my colour. You don't mind.

But somehow I feel
Left out
From a club where You only have
The membership cards

Like a hungry person
In a supermarket,
I watch you buying
Canned fruit
Marked South Africa
And quite honestly
(hungry or not)
I don't want peaches
In black blood.

Peaches in black blood
Would taste like corpse in my mouth.

THURSDAY 13 NOVEMBER
1980

Masturbation – Public meeting.

SATURDAY 15 NOVEMBER
1980

Anti-sexist party.

THURSDAY 4 DECEMBER
1980

British Movement posters put up (about me!!). English: Yeats
essay back 'A'.

FRIDAY 17 JULY
1981

Going out with Gloria 8.00 at The Oval.
Attacked by fascists at The Angel.

WEDNESDAY 22 JULY

1981

Black man at tube station. Drunk. Shouting 'do you love black people?' looking at me. Desperate drunk eyes. Gives 10p to a white baby. Stares and stares at me. Talks about his people, his home. Shouts he hates Britain.

THURSDAY 23 JULY

1981

Went to see Biko Inquest. Met man from Zimbabwe.

FRIDAY 21 AUGUST

1981

Went to Olivette's. Had beautiful meal that her mother had prepared. Ingrid there too. Later, Olivette and Ingrid played music then I read them 'Reflections'. Never had an audience like them – it was so beautiful to find black women identifying with what I'd written. Olivette was stunned speechless. Then we all went to Mo's. It was lovely to see Mo, felt like I hadn't seen her for ages. Mo, George and I sat up and talked till 4 in the morning, Mo cried about all the years of waste and giving. We talked about our perceptions of each other.

SATURDAY 22 AUGUST

1981

Party. Amazing. 25 black lesbians dancing, laughing, smiling. Olivette wrote and gave me a poem about me and I cried because it was so touching. Sheila and Pam gave me a lovely card. Ingrid a cuddle like I've never had before.

MONDAY 24 AUGUST

1981

Leaving for the holidays. Rushed around all day doing things in town. Met Ingrid at the squat, then we went for a meal in West Kensington. Had a good talk with each other. I really love Ingrid.

Then we went to the writers' group – last one in a while.
Got my new name – oh! AKANKE IFE
Discussed 'Reflections'. Said a sad goodbye.

SATURDAY 12 SEPTEMBER

1981

Went round to Mo's for about two. Mo and I talked for a while alone – lovely seeing her. Then Jocelyn came. Lots of upsetting things with Gregory and everybody making demands on Mo. Jocelyn had a broken nose. We all sat and talked and laughed and I felt really high. Went to bed, slept in Mo's room for cuddles and comfort. Mo – really warm and loving. Went to sleep at three. Both of us had weird dreams.

SUNDAY 13 SEPTEMBER

1981

Woke up and talked with Mo – about having a white woman
as your best friend – energising, wish we had longer,
just beginning to relax with each other. She saw me off.
Reluctantly left for Big Isolation Town [*Stirling*].

THURSDAY 29 OCTOBER

1981

Ingrid and Olivette arrived! Can't believe they're here. Spent
morning catching up on what's been going on. Everything
absolutely lovely, had nice meal and talked and talked sitting
round the log fire – cosy. Then read poems to each other.
Ingrid read this poem about Jocelyn. They liked 'Blacker and
Blacker' [*Jackie's short story about a black girl who scrubbed
her skin to make herself white*] and killed themselves
laughing, tears splashing at 'White Rose'. Talked about guilt
about feeling not right-on enough, and lack of confidence
about being anglicised. About Olivette's mother saying to her
it's too late to change now. About suicide.

Talked about looks and how we see ourselves. Ingrid
felt more relaxed than she has done, speaking about all her
anxieties and the feeling of saying the wrong things. Olivette
talked about that too. We're all really close, hugged lots.
Talked and laughed a lot.

Showed them the fascist posters. Ugh. Oh, Olivette and
Ingrid think I have got a strong face!

1 THURSDAY (152-213)
Corpus Christi

Had History first Period. Miss Mont told me off about my corrections. Then English Comprehension. Lat. we did some irregular verbs. French we read Tartuffe. Games we were in the Gym as it was raining all afternoon. We fought, argued and bullied then all went up to the Det. Geet. the proposed a completion between house 6th Y. 4th form here in the Chilterns. Received with general enthusiasm. Had my Y. before 7.30 read until about went to bed at 10 o'clock.

2 FRIDAY (153-212)

Had Eng. Just read they German. After Break we had Bio. and I was back in Mrs Pope good books. At dinner time somebody pinched my sandwiches in ad to go down to Harrow Weald or something. We worked out our groups for the athletics. We Occasions and Stokes. Sports is on Jan 24th from Great Missenden Station. Had 3 long lessons in the afternoon. French, Girls Geog. Did you discus, standard "A" and javelin "B". Before going changed to 0" at the discus. Goodbye late. Didn't go to G's watched tele as I have bad cough and cold. Bed late.

3 SATURDAY (154-211)

Got up quite early. Did a little shopping. Had dinner then started to do a french C.C. Pope finished it early and went and helped Harold clean the car. In the evening Corinne & Harold went round to an old school friend's house and Mart came round and Jeff and Shirley, Jeff Mart & I went to a party as well. Got in late.

MICHAEL ROSEN

Michael Rosen is a children's poet, former Children's Laureate, journalist and broadcaster. He is the author of over 140 books, including the classic We're Going on a Bear Hunt *and* Michael Rosen's Sad Book, *inspired by the sudden death of his son Eddie in 1999. His memoir,* So They Call You Pisher!, *was published in 2017.*

I was 14 going into 15 and decided that I was sensitive. To prove that I was sensitive I would keep a diary. The only drawback here is that I wasn't sensitive. Another project I had with the diary was that I would be honest. Again, that had a drawback: I couldn't tell myself the truth. Neither of these situations proved to be an obstacle, and the diary is full of gross boasts and fibs. As I read it, I really can't find much resemblance between what I know really happened and what I say happened. There's ludicrous stuff about going down the boozer and getting drunk or convincing girls that I was clever. I was genuinely excited that I could get into a pub and not get thrown out for being underage, but I hated the taste of beer. I don't think I ever convinced any girls that I was clever or, if I did, it was further evidence for them as to why best to steer clear of me. You would never know from the diary that I didn't have a girlfriend until about six months after I gave up writing it. I guess I gave up because even I could peer through the self-deceit and see that it was boloney.

My advice to myself at that time would be, in very polite terms, to make less noise. As my father used to say, 'We come into the countryside for a bit of peace and quiet and all we can hear is mad Michael shouting his bloody head off.' He had a point.

TUESDAY 10 JANUARY

1961

Michael is 14.

Back to school.

Christ! What a dump. Yesterday I thought that school would be all right, and really I was looking forward to it. But I woke up this morning and I felt just like people say they feel the morning after getting boozed. I really hated going back and seeing so many phonies.

WEDNESDAY 11 JANUARY

1961

All the teachers smile at me and talk to me as if I was their buddy or something. Miss Williams asked if I was okay after being ill. Roberts told me how to do maths. Miss Jems told me she would help me get a library book out. McKenzie read my copy of *Punch*. Hoppy told me I was doing well at PE ... I don't know, it must be some new scheme of theirs to try and stop me mucking about. I suppose it has succeeded. At last they've worked out how to deal with me – damn!

I had an argument with some girls in my form – a political one: for and against the H bomb. I skilfully indoctrinated them. I need a haircut. I toughed a chap up for bashing me with his bike.

THURSDAY 12 JANUARY
1961

A pretty dull day. I have come to the conclusion that in the 4th form there are no girls to whom one could talk to about anything. They are either geniuses and frightful to look at, or typical middle school girls that think they are more intelligent than boys. That annoys me, that attitude. I defeated it today in two girls by talking a) about politics and b) using grown up words. It slayed them. I am generally cheesed off. I have scarcely done a stroke for the exams.

SATURDAY 14 JANUARY
1961

Went into Harrow in the afternoon – bought record player deck and a pair of shoes for me. I've been thinking about the people in my form, their attitude to life and so on. I think it is to do with sociology and it interests me quite a bit. Arsenal won 5–4.

FRIDAY 20 JANUARY
1961

Went to the library in the morning and got two history books out. After dinner I watches Wales v England – Wales won 6–3. Did not do any work, got Geoggers on Monday. I'm to worry! Pater bought a dead snazzy new coat. All woolly and spotty. Saw the inauguration of Kennedy on BBC 10.45pm (GMT) It was a farce. Went to bed pretty late.

THURSDAY 26 JANUARY
1961

Felt fantastically rotten when woke up in the morning. Sore throat, headache and temp. Cos I went to bed late, both Pater and Mum went out house saying it was cos I never go to bed early. Bri [*Brian, Michael's older brother*] looked after me as P and M at work.

FRIDAY 27 JANUARY
1961

Felt real rotten, stayed in bed again all day and did nothing. Doc came. I have got tonsillitis. Bri got prescription and I was nearly sick with the gargle and the pills he gave me.

SATURDAY 28 JANUARY
1961

Ill still, but better. Dead boring in bed.

SATURDAY 4 FEBRUARY
1961

I am considering a youth hostel tour of Radnorshire at Easter. I got two books out of the library on it.

THURSDAY 9 FEBRUARY

1961

I am ill again. I got up early, feeling like, and looking like, a 'lucky-I-didn't-tread-in-it'. I was then encouraged to go back to bed and consequently was forgotten. Pater, Frater, and Mater all left without saying goodbye or anything and I read, slept and thought until mum got in at 6. They were a bit annoyed I was ill again but it was OK. Had two aspirins and sweated like stink. Mum says that it is my way of curing myself. Huh!

FRIDAY 10 FEBRUARY

1961

I do feel better. I'm a bit annoyed I'm ill and so on. Listened to wireless quite a bit. Mum was at home because of half term. She went for an interview to the Institute in the morning about a course on Primary Education. I sit ill in bed and do nothing. I am a real big shot. I feel a lot better in fact. Could get up. Don't. Typical. Bri comes upstairs beats me up and then says he is tired. Apparently he had to go to the hospital to have some glass from chemistry taken out of his finger. It's better now.

FRIDAY 24 FEBRUARY

1961

Late in school again!!

WEDNESDAY 1 MARCH

1961

Got to school late but Stafford was on duty and did not put me down. Mucked about in Latin and Horner got annoyed. Was in fits of laughter during a McKenzie prep and we expected to get a detention but we didn't. Chiz! Instead got 50 lines from Mrs Young.

SUNDAY 2 APRIL

1961

Aldermaston [*the Atomic Weapons Research Establishment, which was the focus of anti-nuclear rallies*]

Got up dead early. Mum had very kindly made my sandwiches. I got a train to Uxbridge and then a bus to Slough. Wandered about with the other 20,000 and then found Bri. Sang songs and then mucked about and got in dead beat.

MONDAY 3 APRIL

1961

Slept like a log. Pater took us to Turnham Green by car. Pouring with rain the whole time. Ate dinner in Kensington Gardens. After dinner made friends with Hig's sister and her friends. Hig's sister and I went off together and I held her hand. She was terrific. Seeing her at party on Thursday. Rally was stupendous – Whitehall was thick and Trafalgar Square jammed.

SATURDAY 6 MAY

1961

Had huge tea. Chris came round with Jeff's girl – Jo. Listened to loads of jazz that Jo brought round. Got a pair of green suede shoes for my birthday present. They go really well with my twill trousers. Bed 11 o'clock.

SUNDAY 7 MAY

1961

My birthday

Thought I was staying in bed till late – got up and found I was the first. Bri gave me three books and Pater gave me a pound note. Posted leaflets in the morning. Homework in the afternoon.

WEDNESDAY 24 MAY

1961

Got up quite early and spend the whole day at Pinner Fair. Spent about 5/-. Won a coconut. Fiddled a fruit machine and it emptied itself on us. Gave some girls the eye. Bought a hot dog. Met Brio, saw Judith's sister, Leyla, Richard Jones and millions of others. Met Mr Evans while chatting up some girl. He said 'seducing the local virgins eh, Rosen?' Had a couple of rides on the dodgems before prices went up. Bed late. Feeling jolly tired.

SHEILA HANCOCK

Sheila Hancock CBE *is an actress and author, born on the Isle of Wight in 1933. She is known for her work on stage and television, notably in* Cabaret, Entertaining Mr Sloane, The Winter's Tale, The Rag Trade *and* Sweeney Todd.

Harriet Jaine, producer of My Teenage Diary: Sheila Hancock's diaries are special. They describe a momentous time in the young Sheila's life – her first trip abroad; her first dance; her first kiss; her first sighting of a bikini – and they are beautifully written. They transport the reader back to another time, when Europe was just emerging from the dark days of war.

Hancock was just 14 when she embarked on this adventure to France completely on her own, to stay with a French family. The trip was organised by a French teacher, and Sheila kept a diary of her travels so that her parents would know what she had got up to: 'I decided that I was going to keep a record of it because my mum and dad had had to cough up £10 for the trip.'

This holiday to France was transformative for Sheila Hancock. Her visit to the town of Royan, which had been razed to the ground by Allied forces, made her into a lifelong pacifist convinced of 'the idiocy of war'. The holiday also gave her new-found self-confidence – she blossomed. I will always remember the hush in the studio as Hancock read out her final entry. 'Oh! what a holiday,' she said. 'There will be no holiday like my first adventure abroad. I wasn't the same girl there, I was – well, I don't know if it was the real me or not, but I was a grown-up individual. I think this holiday was a glimpse of the future Sheila.'

SATURDAY 30 JULY

1947

Sheila is 14.

Phew! Here I am at last on the train.

We started this morning at 10 o'clock by nearly missing the train from Bexleyheath. We went to the bank and then had hours to spare much to dad's fury. However, we wandered to Buckingham Palace, saw the changing of the guard and rested in St James's Park. Dad's anger was pacified a little when he was able to watch two girls who were practically in the nude.

Eventually we got to the station and the train was an hour late. Gosh, what a flap! The thing I am most concerned about is dad – he must have aged years!

Any rate, dad, I appreciate it and love you for it; although I seemed ultra-cool I was only trying to comfort you and show you I was all right! I do hope this trip's not going to be terribly expensive. I vow I'll get a job and do all I can to cover my keep at least. The collector has just taken part of my ticket. Yippee I'm on my way!

MONDAY 1 AUGUST

1947

I went round Paris seeing the sights. Tasted first French food. Wonderful. We had entrees of egg and ham pie concoction then rabbit beautifully cooked then potato salad, then French beans, then sweet, then *Pain* and cheese, then fruit, then coffee, and, of course, wine all the time. It is bitter and queer but lovely. You can have it with water but it's much nicer neat.

I also had spirit (you dip sugar in) ... this was too strong for my liking however.

THURSDAY 4 AUGUST
1947

I am at the moment lying on the beach roasting, watching all the people. Never have I seen people so brown. They are almost black. They hardly wear anything at all. The briefer the suits, the better they seem to like it. Dad would be in his element. The young folk are terribly good looking. I think it must be their brown skin and many have jet black, shiny hair. And they are all so completely happy. The French people are charming.

WEDNESDAY 13 AUGUST
1947

Yesterday I went to Royan. This used to be a huge town with many huge picturesque houses. In 1945, just before the Germans in France surrendered, the allied planes suddenly came upon Royan. For two hours there was hell on earth during which the whole town was razed to the ground. When I say whole town, I mean it. I have never seen anything so terrible in all my life. Imagine the bomb damage we saw in Canterbury increased to a hundred or more times in size. You can stand and look at mile and miles of ruins. Thousands of people were killed.

All this would not be so terrible if it had been to some purpose, but it wasn't. The British have admitted it was a terrible mistake – there are notices up saying 'this town was destroyed by mistake' and it was done just 2 days before the surrender … I don't know how they could ever forgive us. I was awfully glad to leave. It had a terrible atmosphere of death, it almost seemed to whisper accusingly 'Why? Why?' I stood looking at the ground with odd walls silhouetted against that blue sky. I feel I wanted to say that there should never be another war. I'd like to take all the politicians and war mongers to that place and say 'look, this is the sort of thing you're responsible for. You ruin beauty, you kill – we ordinary folk are the ones who suffer. Why don't you grow up and realise what's at stake?'

THURSDAY 14 AUGUST
1947

I've been on the beach today having a wonderful time. A word on the French boys, which is a trifle embarrassing – French males are always on the lookout for good-looking females, and if they find one they don't hesitate to tell everyone what they think! And another thing – French boys are so different to the English. Firstly, they make friends so quickly. In England they would be called 'fresh' and girls might think they weren't very nice, but here it's just natural. If you are all alone it's not long before several boys are talking to you – perfectly nice, sensible boys too. They are *extremely* polite, it's quite thrilling to be with them because they are so polite and seemingly doting on you!

SATURDAY 27 AUGUST

1947

We went to a café here for dancing. Up to now I've been petrified to dance but they made me and I thoroughly enjoyed it. The band consists of students who are earning a bit of money in the holiday. They are all quite mad and one is like Danny Kaye. A whole lot of students frequent the place and it's an absolute uproar. They all wear jeans and bright plaid shirts hanging outside. They dance mad to Bebop tunes and sing student songs. I simply adore the place. Everyone is so friendly. I danced with several people, 'Danny Kaye' included. I had a smashing time.

By the way, since I've been here everyone offers me cigarettes and I've always refused. Now they say that I will appear rude if I continue and they bought a packet of weak ones just for me. The first time I nearly choked but now I occasionally have one and quite enjoy it but I'm by no means mad about it. I am slowly going downhill I'm afraid!

Have become very friendly with the band at the promenade, especially 'Danny'. Yesterday we left the café at about 2 o'clock and Danny followed us and came home with us. When we got to the gate he suggested a 'walk'.

Now, Mum and Dad, I don't want you to be cross, I want you to try and understand. It was the sort of wonderful night that you only find here; I wasn't a bit tired. It was wonderful – 'Danny' is a terribly nice boy and I'm sure you wouldn't mind if you knew what a lovely time I had. He acted the fool the whole time – really he could go a long way on the stage. He danced, he sang, he gave speeches to the sky. I'd love you to meet him; he reminds me of you dad sometimes, in his ways.

I'd better add that I intend to go to bed early tonight to make up for lost sleep.

***

This holiday really has done me no end of good because, although I know it doesn't always seem like it, I know I have a sort of inferiority complex. That, I think, is why I've never liked dancing. But here no end of people have asked me to dance – and not only once – which shows I wasn't too bad the first time. What has bucked up my ego no end is that the boys of the band have danced with me, and all the girls run after them like mad.

I've been awfully glad since I've been here that I am typically English to look at. Nobody has been disappointed because I seem to be their ideal of English women! Except as far as clothes are concerned, they all expect old fashioned tweeds and shorts to my knees, whereas here I wear my shorts rolled right up, my sunsuit without straps and my blue blouse right off my shoulders. I wear a little curly fringe which is most becoming and the perm is a tremendous success. I am a nice golden brown and although I know my features never were and never will be very hot – I really look very attractive, at least I think the French boys think so!

***

I'm feeling terribly sad today because the boys parted this morning. I had grown terribly fond of them especially Claude. I loathe making friends and then having to say goodbye. I know I shall probably never see any of that crowd again and

I feel thoroughly depressed. I suppose when I get away from Fouras the harsh reminders will be gone and I shall have only pleasant – oh so very pleasant – memories.

Oh! what a holiday. There will be no holiday like my first adventure abroad. I wasn't the same girl there, I was – well, I don't know if it was the real me or not, but I was a grown-up individual. I think this holiday was a glimpse of the future Sheila.

It's so difficult to explain, perhaps you understand, but it's much more likely that you don't.

Anyway, I'm so grateful to mummy and daddy for making that 6 weeks of heaven – yes, heaven – possible.

DATE 22nd August   DAY Tuesday 1978

This is when I got my diary.
I got it from my pen pal in Boston
Mass, her name is pamela maine.
She sent it to me for my birthday
which is September 27th. It arrived
in the morning when I was at school
So my Auntie Kay gave it to me in
the Afternoon as they are looking after
me while my mum and Dad are
away on holiday in the caravan.

DATE 23rd August   DAY Wednesday
I got up in the morning and went
to school. Came home at lunch time
and went back to school. After I went
up to the post office to post my pen
pal letter but the man at the
post office (GRUMP) wouldn't let me
post it so I had to come all the way
down again.

RHONA CAMERON

Rhona Cameron is a writer and comedian. Born in Dundee in 1965, she was adopted as a baby and brought up in the small fishing town of Musselburgh, East Lothian. She has authored two books, her first a memoir 1979: A Big Year in a Small Town contains her diary extracts. She shot to fame winning Channel 4's So You Think You're Funny competition at the Edinburgh Festival in 1992 and became the first openly gay woman in the UK to have her own show, the sitcom Rhona *she co-penned and starred in.*

I was 13 years old when my first 'official' diary arrived from my American pen pal. I was initially disappointed because it had a silly picture of a lady with a long dress on the front cover, but inside it quickly became my confidant, my confession.

The year 1978 was pivotal for me and the entire country; awful events were just around the corner and, by the end of 1979, my father would be dead. A lot of the reference to my sexuality was influenced by the Jeremy Thorpe trial at the time, which was the first depiction of homosexuality I had encountered.

The style and content of the writing is not entirely free, it's measured and deliberate – formal even – mixed with deliberate attempts at humour. I think I had a strong sense that in my future it might be read. I had an innate feeling that I was a storyteller, a John-Boy Walton character, destined to leave the persecutory misery of the small town for broader horizons. A lost complicated soul trying to process life's pain through the art of story.

I come from a church background, with very old-fashioned war generation parents, so I had an innocence that comes through in the writing, and a concern for the 'moral values' I'd had drummed into me. This became intensely complex when my irrepressible lesbianism started to dominate my life. I was bullied and blackmailed at school, which made my loneliness unbearable around the time of my father's deterioration and death. At this time, my diary was a place to retreat to, a place to document the turmoil and misery of my situation.

Inside the front cover of Rhona's diary:
What is written in this diary is the whole truth and the way I feel in occasions in life.

16/7/79: This is full of special stages in adolescence, some good, and mostly bad.

13/3/80: Please if you have read this, hold none of the contents against me. Please I had to explain the following important stages, verified in this book.

TUESDAY 22 AUGUST

1978

Rhona is 12.

This is when I got my diary.

I got it from my pen pal in Boston, Massachusetts. Her name is Pamela Maine.

She sent it to me for my birthday which is September 27th. It arrived in the morning when I was at school so my Auntie Kay gave it to me in the afternoon as they are looking after me while my mum and dad are away on holiday in the caravan.

FRIDAY 25 AUGUST

1978

Today was the best day of all – after school Jennifer and I went to Guides and next to the Guide Hall round the back is an old house with a garden, with pear and apple trees leaning over. Captain told us to collect leaves but instead me and a few others went and picked pears and ate the ripe ones but Captain gave us a row.

On the way home from Guides we saw Stewart rushing out of his house and he shouted to us and pointed up to the sky. We looked up and we saw a UFO. It was smaller than a plane and it had white lights all round with a red light at the top. It was flying low and it swirled round and back and forward making a hovering sound. But no one believed us but it's true.

THURSDAY 21 DECEMBER
1978

On Thursday evening I was supposed to meet Michele and Lynn at the Brunton Hall at 7.00pm to go to Christmas disco. I had previously told my dad it was strictly fifteen years and under and that it would be well catered for and quiet. It turned out to be the most rowdy lot of shit I had ever been to. When we all met they dragged me into the toilets which was occupied by eight 16-year-old big chested girls combing their hair, some smoking and others having a good slosh of McEwans Export until they were sick. All they spoke about was what happened when they went out with the boys. The conversation and behaviour was out of line, not that I'm an angel, but I felt so clean and sacred compared to them.

I bumped into Hilary and she seemed to be stoned but she was only putting it on. How could anyone be on 2 bottles of cider that they bought at the Co-op?

I went back to talking to Shona. I'd heard rumours about her, folk saying she was cheap. By now I could strangle whoever said that. The music was a sound version of Concorde taking off. You couldn't hear yourself shout. Finally it all finished, I got Shona downstairs and said I would see her in the holidays and she agreed. Well my dad picked me up and we went home. I felt rather giddy.

FRIDAY 22 DECEMBER

1978

This was a memorable day. It was the last day of term. I woke up with a head like a steel box. I walked to school and decided to start it by going a walk in the graveyard. It was a cold, foggy morning and the graveyard quiet and undisturbed suited the somewhat gruesome weather. I walked around the graveyard for one hour. I followed the steps that Alison and I walked one year ago. A tear ran down my face when I thought of her.

When I went back to English the class neglected me so I walked around the corridors. Later at 11.30am it was the school service with that poofish minister who didn't find the slightest thing funny. But when he was boring us to death his microphone took a relapse and he sounded like Sid Vicious singing 'The bells of Saint Martins'. Then it came to the choir and Alison was in it. She was still the same as she had been for a month. I decided to tell her my long and sad speech after school. It was strange seeing all the school and the staff together. Seeing people I used to speak to. I started to cry but wiped my eyes and joined in the songs.

Afterwards I asked Louise where Alison was and she had gone to get a lift home.

I came home thinking about Alison and thinking how much I would miss her at Christmas.

SUNDAY 31 DECEMBER
1978

'The below statement is a solemn promise.'

I am entering this in my diary at 11.51pm, 9 minutes before 1979. I want to forget the past and live in the present and the future. I no longer am the past Rhona Campbell because I am hopefully going to leave her at 12.00. I dread school but I am going to try and forget Alison as she hates me. I am going to be more refined, calm, cool, obedient and all the other things that make a respectable human being. Amen.

MONDAY 1 JANUARY
1979

This year Christmas has been very dull. Before, when I was friends with Alison, I was the happiest person in town and I wanted to be with everyone and have fun. I had lots of friends and everything was fine. But then Alison wouldn't listen to me, so I had to turn to other friends, at least that was what I called them. They spread it about and Alison got called names as well but I took most. Finally, I knew it would happen, one day after school we met and she said –

'don't go in a huff but I don't want to have anything to do with you.' And I asked her if she hated me and she said yes. After that I begged her to come back but she said no. I drank and drank and grew grumpy and bad tempered and sad. And now I just want to be on my own so you see this year has been hell.

FRIDAY 29 JUNE
1979

Today was the last day of term. I broke my nose when I was playing in the park. Karen got me home and she gave me a poem about love or something. It was crap so I just ripped it up.

Later, I was sad to leave Susan. I went to the hospital and I saw Susan when I came back. I'm not a Homosexual but I admit I do have homosexual feelings and tendencies towards Susan but I'm not queer.

THURSDAY 11 OCTOBER
1979

I've found a cure: boys. If I'm to go out with a boy I really like, I forget about Lisa or Susan or anyone else I'm attracted to. I was pleased when I got to school – I really felt great and I like David more than ever. But as usual I shot my mouth off. I feel depressed and I'm still liking Lisa. I'm obsessed with her.

WEDNESDAY 11 NOVEMBER
1979

Today is a day I will remember for the rest of my life. My dad has been taken ill and been put in hospital 3 days ago. His condition was getting slowly worse.

My dad has been ill for a year, and yesterday my mum broke down in tears, for an unknown reason. Today she told me that my own dad whom I love with great respect has bone cancer (due to smoking) and he is going to die in a while. He does not know it. But now I would give up everything for my dad to be well again for I love him now more than I've ever done before. I told my mum today that she must promise never to cry again!!

My dad (said my mum) thought he was well and was looking bright today, but, despite that, the odds are 100–1 he's going to die. I am going to try everything to save him. I'm praying, sticking in at school. And most of all hoping that he will live. I love my dad.

FRIDAY 23 NOVEMBER
1979

Today is the most important day of my life, because at 1.00pm this afternoon my mum informed me that my dad had died at 10.05am this morning. He had taken a relapse in the Northern Hospital and died in a coma. As his heartbeat faded away. He was in no pain, and didn't know that he had cancer.

If he had of lived he would eventually die soon in pain. And I'm thankful, in fact we all are, that he wasn't in pain. (My teachers and friends were wonderful.)

SUNDAY 25 DECEMBER
1979

Today was Christmas day. It was very sad and lonely without my dad but I got lots of presents and everyone was wonderful. All the family came down as usual and we had a meal. (And the usual routine, the only exception was my dad.)

21-3-97 China? 11-25-96 AM

O.K, it's quite a confusing time right now (11:00 pm if you're interested). It's Friday night, and and I've got a belly full of beer. Surprisingly I don't really feel drunk but that's probably just the contrast to Phil who is frankly pissed. I've had an odd week. I've been trying to 'phone C but have not got through — I even tryed to send her a telegram. Carol, on the other hand — I have spoken to twice and the recurring protestations of

ALEX
HORNE

Alex Horne is a comedian and writer, the creator of comedy panel show Taskmaster *and of* The Horne Section, *a Radio 4 music variety show. Born in 1978, Horne studied at Cambridge, where he was a member of Footlights.*

My diary covers the time in my life that I am least proud of. I was officially a grown up, I was living away from my parents, but I was acting like a child. I'd never reread the entries before the *My Teenage Diary* radio show. My memories were foggy; a vague awareness that I'd been an enormous prat. I'd also never thrown the diaries away so perhaps I was always going to sneak a peek at some point.

I'm glad I wrote down how I was feeling at the time, even if it makes me want to never leave the house again. I stopped writing a diary when I left university and now I wish I'd carried on. Perhaps I will. Because even though the person who wrote those words was apparently one of the worst people in the world, he still made me laugh, he still made some good decisions and he's still my children's dad.

I haven't decided if I'll ever let them read the rest of the diaries. I haven't read any more of them myself yet. It's one of those situations when it's actually less embarrassing to read them out loud on national radio than to do it all by yourself.

After leaving China I went to New Zealand where I got a tattoo of a lizard on my arm. It's no work of art. It's imperfect, misjudged and unsightly, like most of my gap year behaviour. But I love my lizard and I loved my time in China – 21 years later, I have no regrets.

SUNDAY 23 FEBRUARY

1997

Alex is 18.

Phil and I are continually putting off preparing our lessons. I've got to teach class 1 at 7.40 tomorrow morning and I've just decided to concentrate on descriptions. I really think I'd better get down to that now, actually. Well, maybe after a bit of lie-down.

Some thoughts: 1. The Chinese don't all wear glasses, hardly any here in Quanzhou in fact. 2. Might try jogging sometime. 3. The Chinese are v active. Whether it's tai-chi, sprinting, football, basketball, or just stretching and jogging, they all do something and they're all fit. Apart from the Buddhas, I've never seen a fat Chinaman. They eat a lot though. Constantly. 4. I must put some sun cream on.

MONDAY 24 FEBRUARY

1997

Just done first lesson. Crikey it was difficult. I really came unstuck and ended up learning Chinese instead. Still, I have learnt something and will now try to prepare the next one.

TUESDAY 25 FEBRUARY

1997

The second lesson went swimmingly, well most of it. A couple of spine-tingling moments when they spontaneously applauded me for trying to speak their language. Also managed to sing 'Yesterday' with the class. Anyway, I got on very well with the students and later received 14 eggs as a present. (I'd managed to slip in that we were short of eggs.) Actually, I was on the toilet when I heard a knock on the door, behind which 5 girls stood eagerly awaiting my presence. Anyway, we're now getting used to these visits, most of which are interesting and enjoyable.

Today is Deng Xiao Ping's funeral and our timetable is changed. The students are going to watch the event but don't really seem to care.

WEDNESDAY 26 FEBRUARY

1997

My left ear has grown immeasurably (I have no ruler). It has swollen up and turned purple. It no longer resembles my right ear. What the heck is going on? Excuse me, why is my ear so big? I look like a mutant and feel like one too. Quite funny to an extent but if it doesn't go down soon I'll cut it off. Hear that buster? I'll cut you off.

SUNDAY 9 MARCH

1997

My ear is back to normal.

We've got a routine going now – teaching, eating, sleeping, and sport. Also, the people who visit the flat have been narrowed down to a mere 20 odd. We have about 5 people around every other night. Some have incredible English – but some are just terrible.

SATURDAY 15 MARCH

1997

At last I wake. V.H.O. [*very hung over*]. Got very drunk last night. Drinking from 3 till 3 is not good for sobriety. And, dear-oh dear, managed to pull a Chinese girl. A real, genuine, Chinese girl. How? Why? Who? Mmm ... what heck do? Her name is May – v good at English, quite attractive, v interesting and amusing. She knows about Christine, she understands, she's very cool, oh dear I'm really v hung over and I'll see her tonight.

TUESDAY 18 MARCH

1997

Spoke to Christine twice yesterday, making me feel a little guilty about what happened with May, but cheering me up too. I think I'll see her soon.

I'm in a bit of a quandary right now woman-wise. I'll give you the facts:

1. Christine says she loves me and wants to know how I feel.
2. Danielle is waiting for me back home.
3. May is waiting for me to phone and write, as well as come and see her soon.
4. Sally Jones is stalking me.

I think I'm going to be brave. I'll phone May on Thursday and tell her I can't be more than friends. She's a sensible girl so she should hate me, with a bit of luck. Danielle knows I'll mess around and she probably will too. Sally – I could probably avoid seeing. Christine is definitely the one, but whether I can tell her what she wants to hear is another thing. What heck do? Have a shower. Yeah.

MONDAY 24 MARCH
1997

Stupid, insensitive fool. Yes, you, Al, you piece of crap. I have just called May and tried to dump her, but she was engaged (unfortunately not to a man). She's apparently gone mental. She sent me a telegram (just 'Alex' on the address) with the words 'miss you terribly' printed in the middle. What have I done? I've created a monster. I've worked out a reasonably sound speech to tell her, but over the phone? What a creep. I don't know how she's going to react, especially when I've told her that she could stay this weekend (what was I thinking?).

The trouble is that I don't feel anything about May now – she is not a beauty and I was *very* drunk.

WEDNESDAY 21 MAY
1997

OK. Before inventing the most famous of all mints, Marco Polo wrote – 'Grand and beautiful, Quanzhou is one of the greatest ports of the world.' Nowadays you have to look very hard to find Quanzhou in a travel book (and if you do succeed, it will probably contain the words 'drab', 'dull', and 'don't go there'). Quanzhou does not do itself justice. Streets lined with blossoming trees overflow with litter, while honking motorbikes swarm around the temples. However, it is those environmentally unconscious litterers that give Quanzhou its real beauty.

If your ever come to Quanzhou, look deep into the town and you'll see the colour, the oddities, the happiness, and above all, the beauty. Dreams are never fulfilled and lives are limited but show me a country where this is not the case. Here no one moans about what they haven't got but they make the best of what they do have. I'm very proud to live in a place like Quanzhou.

My life here is very different from in England but I love it. Just in case you're interested, since I arrived I've eaten pig's lung, intestine and face, chicken's feet, turtle's blood, frog's legs, raw cray fish, giant woodlice, fish eyes, whole dove, squid, snails and strawberries.

THURSDAY 22 MAY

1997

We got given bikes today – Bert and Ernie – so that'll add another degree of independence. And I got a letter from Mum and a note from Dad. Mum writes me these really long letters full of detail and feeling – I've never read anything like this from her before and it's amazing – she just seems like a really close friend – not like a mum at all – it's brilliant and I've kind of seen a side of her that I hadn't really appreciated before. I guess it's the fault of us four blokes that means she hasn't been able to express herself all the time.

She's sending the *Blues Brothers* video over. Yippee!

SATURDAY 24 MAY

1997

Alcohol abuse and theft on a grand scale have been the main themes of the last two days. I don't know why we keep stealing things but when we're pissed it seems like fun. Here's a brief list of what we've got – a broom, 3 stools, 5 glasses, forks, knives, spoons, ashtray, chopsticks and holders, loo roll dispenser, a lock from a door, brake fluid and oil tank, bowls, plates, toilet flusher, and two toilet seats. Those seats were taken yesterday and were transported in my trousers. Hell, we were drunk yesterday.

WEDNESDAY 11 JUNE

1997

Good evening. I'm looking forward to my last lesson, ever. It's tonight – we'll just be doing music and we're going to take the *Blues Brothers* (which we watched again last night) so the lesson will be pretty relaxed. We've been promised a good time afterwards courtesy of Mr Yang, so Thursday could well be brought to you by the letters V, H and the number O. Last lesson at the college this morning. Sort of sad, sort of bloody happy. They gave me a card, so that was nice.

TUESDAY 17 JUNE

1997

But it's all over now. I've left Quanzhou exactly four months after we arrived in China. Here I am sitting in a very stationary bus somewhere. It's 4.24pm and I've got something in my eye.

January 9

1971 Went shopping in the early morning, at HARRODs expecting it to be practicly empty, infact it was **packed. Still.** After lunch KATY took me too see Sadlers Wells, apen then for dinner at her place. The opera was o.k but not fantastic, I must start slimming on Monday

19

19

19

19

ARABELLA WEIR

Arabella Weir is a British comedian, actor and writer. Born in 1957, she was part of the ground-breaking comedy sketch troupe behind The Fast Show, *and wrote and performed the classic sketch 'Does my bum look big in this?' She also created and starred in the TV series* Posh Nosh.

Re-reading these teenage diaries I experience an equal mix of excruciating embarrassment at how lah-di-dah I was, and painful recall of how insecure and unsure of myself I was. It seems a bit odd now that I could be both. And I can't believe I was so obsessed with my weight – I was young, having a fantastic time, very popular and a great deal thinner than I am now (when I don't care). I now know I wasn't fat at all. But I guess that's what youth is all about. I'm pretty pleased, retrospectively, at my success with boys, because it sure didn't feel like that at the time.

I have no idea why I kept a diary. Perhaps it's always the pastime of the self-obsessed – and I was certainly that. I am pained by reading about how much I wanted my (I now know) divorcing parents to get along. But I'm absolutely delighted and very proud to say that many of the girls at school I mention in the diaries are still my closest friends – nearly 50 years on, I think that's a pretty amazing achievement. I find it interesting and amusing, reading these entries, to realise that my own teenage kids say and think pretty much exactly the same things as I did all those years ago, which only goes to prove that I do know what I'm fucking talking about when they scream at me that I don't!

SATURDAY 9 JANUARY
1971

Arabella is 13.

Went shopping in the early morning at Harrods expecting it
to be practically empty, in fact it was packed full. After lunch
Katy took me to see a Sadler's Wells opera then for dinner
at her place. The opera was ok but not fantastic. I must start
slimming on Monday.

WEDNESDAY 20 JANUARY
1971

Went to school. Organised with Caz to hitchhike to the Lake
District when 14. Mum said no. Got sent out of Latin. I must
concentrate more. Came home did my homework. Mummy
didn't let me watch *Monty Python's Flying Circus* because it
was too late. Went to bed. I have got a cold. Must slim and not
be too bitchy.

SUNDAY 24 JANUARY
1971

I doubt if I will start my periods soon. I watched *Jane Eyre*,
it was terribly good. There's a terrible wind and I'm petrified
of it, it makes eerie sounds and blows the trees around in the
night. Went to bed, I have got a terrible headache.

MONDAY 25 JANUARY
1971

Went to school and had games. Then went home for tea with Carey and Camilla, talked a lot about Katy. I hate her. I must get a bra like Cathy's from Marks and Sparks (Oxford Street) 15/- it's lovely. I watched *Mr Digby Darling*. Then bed. I must slim.

TUESDAY 6 FEBRUARY
1971

Lizzy and I woke up very late and had breakfast and then went down town, had a Wimpy and chips and then saw the *Aristocats* it was really lovely and sweet. Then we went to C&A for a joke but it turned out I bought a £3 woollen midi coat and dress!

SUNDAY 14 MARCH
1971

Woke up at 12.20 and then had BRUNCH – BRUNCH is breakfast and lunch.

TUESDAY 6 APRIL
1971

Aujord'hui je suis allee chez Toby avec Karine et Susan nous fumons beaucoup du dope et plus nous buvons du cidre. Toby a telephoné David Rose e il lui dis que je l'aime et aussi que le premier soir que je got off avec il je faites l'amour avec il. Je ne get off pas DT jamais?!!!

FRIDAY 5 NOVEMBER
1971

Stayed home watched fireworks then went to Toby's got really pissed then onto the Heath for a smoke then to this bloke called Richard's house then home by taxi. I really enjoyed the party.

WEDNESDAY 9 MAY
1973

Had my left ear pierced with Sophie.

TUESDAY 3 JULY
1973

Got suspended from school.

WEDNESDAY 4 JULY
1973

Didn't go to school.

SATURDAY 7 JULY

1973

Steve K's party, got off with Nick M.

FRIDAY 13 JULY

1973

Got off with Jeremy (going out).

WEDNESDAY 18 JULY

1973

Didn't go to school due to suspension.

FRIDAY 20 JULY

1973

Fell off Jeremy's Norton commando.

The next few entries are about the rock band – initially known as the Lilletts, then the Polka Dots, then Bazooka Joe – in which Arabella sang backing vocals. This group also featured Stuart Goddard, who later became avant-garde 1980s megastar Adam Ant.

SATURDAY 24 NOVEMBER
1973

Playing at Prince of Wales – concert went well, got off with Jeremy again, I think I'm not in love with him anymore.

TUESDAY 27 NOVEMBER
1973

Lilletts changed name to Polka Dots.

SATURDAY 1 DECEMBER
1973

Back to Lilletts due to popular demand because of 'absorbing' joke.

FRIDAY 7 DECEMBER
1973

Concert went badly, I sang badly because I was drunk.

SATURDAY 8 DECEMBER

1973

Concert went really well.

SUNDAY 23 DECEMBER

1973

The K's party – really good. Got off with Bill E, had to promise to sleep with him before the end of Jan to get a lift home – hope he forgets.

TUESDAY 5 FEBRUARY

1974

FLU. Didn't go to school or band practice. Danny says he's going to let Claire H. sing 'Danny Angel'. If so, I leave the group.

TUESDAY 12 MARCH

1974

Had my *right* ear pierced. Went to band practice. Slept with Nick B after persuading him not to go and see the *Exorcist*.

WEDNESDAY 13 MARCH

1974

Went to Impressionists, excellent. Slept with Nick.

SATURDAY 16 MARCH

1974

Went to Toby's, had haircut, did exam, went to see a *Macbeth* reading, crap, went home, slept with Nick.

WEDNESDAY 27 MARCH

1974

School then bunked biology, bought pizzas then to see *Jules et Jim*, brilliant film, very exhilarating. Went to Toby's, watched telly, good fun, went home, got drunk. Nick went to King Alfred's school dance I think to get off with some girl.

SATURDAY 6 APRIL

1974

Went to practice, went really well, good fun. Then Nick came then we went to party, got off with Rob C, went to bed at 4am. I got flu.

FRIDAY 12 APRIL

1974

Went to Dan D's party, got really pissed, got off with John E.

SATURDAY 13 APRIL

1974

Woke up, was sick, had practice. Did concert, went really well.

SUNDAY 14 APRIL

1974

Went to Brighton, got pissed, got off with John E. Had really good time. Nick chucked me because John and I had spent all day together.

SATURDAY 7 SEPTEMBER

1974

Left Bazooka Joe, a bit sad but it was getting too heavy and serious and I have to work.

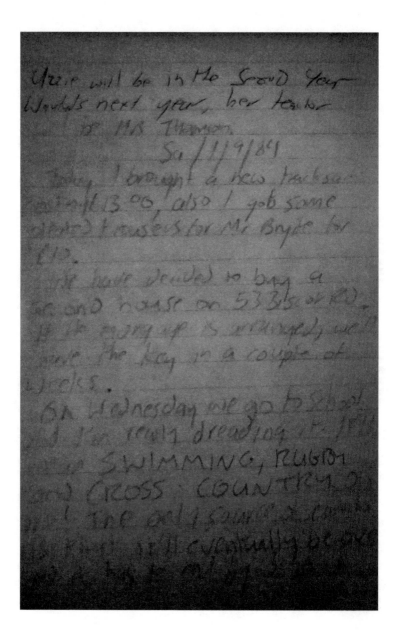

Uzzie will be in the Second Year
Worlds next year, her teacher
is Mrs Thomson.

Su / 1/9/89

Today I brought a new tracksuit
costing £13.00, also I got some
pleated trousers for Mr Bryde for
£12.

We have decided to buy a
second house on 533(?) st Rd.
If the money up is arranged, we
have the key in a couple of
weeks.

On Wednesday we go to School
and I'm really dreading it. I'll
be SWIMMING, RUGBY
and CROSS · COUNTRY. On
the only sport I can
do. It'll eventually be over

SARFRAZ MANZOOR

Sarfraz Manzoor was born in Pakistan in 1971, emigrated to Britain with his family in 1974 and grew up in Luton. He is now a journalist and broadcaster as well as the author of Greetings from Bury Park, *a memoir which tells of his teenage years growing up in Luton and how the music of Bruce Springsteen changed his life. This book has been adapted into a feature film screenplay, called* Blinded by the Light *(2019), directed by Gurinder Chadha.*

I began writing a diary in December 1980 and wrote regularly for the following ten years. In that time I went from being a 9-year-old boy living with my family in Luton to a 19-year-old young man studying in Manchester. I was more honest with my diary than I was with any relative or friend – it was in my diary that I recorded my hopes, dreams and fears. It was a safe place where I could confide. Writing made me feel less alone.

We are expected to feel embarrassed about our teenage diaries but revisiting mine was surprisingly emotional. They reveal how much and how little I have changed. I was reminded of a line from Philip Roth's *American Pastoral*: 'After years and years of painting ourselves opaque this carries us straight back to when we were sure we were transparent.' That is the power of the teenage diary: it offers an unvarnished glimpse into how we really were before the mist of mythologising descended.

When I read my teenage diary it feels like I am being hurled back in time. Suddenly I am a young boy again, obsessed with the pop charts and current affairs and unsure what life has in store. That boy had so many dreams – to live a life less ordinary, to marry someone he loved rather than someone his parents had found – but those dreams felt beyond reach. I wish I could reach across the years and reassure that boy that things would work out, eventually.

SATURDAY 20 DECEMBER

1980

Sarfraz is nine.

I watched *Jungle Book* today. I wonder what it will be like when I'm old. I do not like to think about when I am old for I get scared. I wish I could always stay the same age. I don't want to be 78 or 83.

SATURDAY 7 MAY

1983

It's nearly my birthday. I'm very excited. Latest polls show SDP ahead of Labour.

MONDAY 30 MAY

1983

Today was the Luton Carnival, it was quite good but there were a few skinheads hanging around in groups. The election is going to be held on my birthday June 9th. I will be twelve and all the polls are clearly showing that the Tories have an overwhelming majority. I hope they lose and Labour win. I also hope that when Mum and Dad go to Pakistan they will get my cricket set and also they will get photographs of me when I was little. There has been lots of news since I last wrote. Brezhnev has died and Andropov took his place. My brother took his S level exam on 25th May, his A levels on 28th May. I try to write everyday but sometimes I don't feel like it.

Breakfast TV has begun. I am trying to have a better body since I know my arms aren't very strong. I will try to drink milk every day from now on. 'Candy Girl' by New Edition is number one before that it was 'True' by Spandau Ballet. I have a new bike well second hand from John Bentley for 15 pounds. It's a Grifter. Also, we have bought a Viva for 450 pounds.

TUESDAY 31 MAY
1983

The PM had an interview with Robin Day on *Panorama*. It was good.

THURSDAY 9 JUNE
1983

I am in the dark. Conservatives so far 3 out of 3. I hope they lose. Everyone else is downstairs.

FRIDAY 10 JUNE
1983

Mrs Thatcher won as expected.

THURSDAY 21 JULY
1983

Tomorrow Dad and Mum go to Pakistan. They are going by Gulf Air. I am very sad they are going since I will miss them and feel lonely without their support, help, encouragement and their presence. But since they'll be in Pakistan we might be allowed to go to the cinema and see *The Return of the Jedi* and *Superman III*.

MONDAY 29 AUGUST
1983

Dad went to Pakistan with Mum and they came back on the 14th August one day later than we thought they would. They bought my cricket stuff and lots of ornaments. Dad seems to be on a spending spree (at last) and they have been heard to ask how much a VCR and TV cost.

MONDAY 5 SEPTEMBER
1983

I have learned that we will go to Pakistan in about 2 and a half years' time. I will have good education there and we'll stay for about 4 years. We will take a radio so I can listen to Steve Wright.

MONDAY 31 OCTOBER

1983

We are thinking of getting a computer. I am hoping for an Acorn Electron. Culture Club are number one for the 6th week with 'Karma Chameleon'. America invaded Grenada a few days back. I sometimes wonder if I will get rich, be a millionaire or something like that, I wonder what it feels like to know you can buy all that money can buy, that with a trip down Laskys you can buy a stack system, videodisc and an Apple 1 and still have a few notes in your pocket. Maybe as time goes on my or my brothers' destiny may lead us closer to this dream which all people have, I hope that in coming years we can be justified and have some of the money we deserve, and that in 20 years I could say to mum 'mummy thanks for the hard work you have done and the tender love you have given to me, now relax and don't work any more'. I wish I could repay my family for what they have done to educate me and to be able to say 'you helped me, now I will do something in return.'

Boy George is not number one now it's a crappy song by Billy Joel.

MONDAY 7 NOVEMBER

1983

Channel 4 celebrated its first birthday on Saturday. We are thinking of getting a computer, I think it will be an Acorn Electron with 32KB RAM and 32KB ROM.

FRIDAY 23 DECEMBER
1983

I really hope that we will eventually get a video because then I will be able to get really good films which my mates tell me about like *Zombie Flesh Eaters* and *The Evil Dead*. I spent about 3 hours in town today having a go on the BBC.

MONDAY 26 DECEMBER
1983

Rocky is on but as usual we aren't allowed to watch it. It's such a shame because I haven't anything to do that's why I am in bed. I am so bored not doing anything but writing Urdu and hoovering the kitchen and getting dad's stuff and washing all the dishes and all I flipping get is a 'well done'. At least we could be allowed to see *Rocky* but no. It's always the same I am getting used to it but I am running out of friends since they all say 'did you see this or that?' but I always say 'no' so they don't have anything else to say.

SATURDAY 31 DECEMBER
1983

We hired a video yesterday evening for 24 hours it cost us 5 pounds.

SUNDAY 1 JANUARY

1984

My eyes are getting weaker and smaller, I'm worried that when I grow up to be a doctor I will be blind.

SUNDAY 22 JULY

1984

Yesterday we broke up for the summer holidays. Next term I'll be in the 3rd year. In a way I don't want to be in this year because this means you're growing up and I don't want to grow up.

To me 3rd year sounds really big but I suppose when you get there it won't be that big sounding.

'Two Tribes' by Frankie Goes to Hollywood is number 1.

SATURDAY 1 SEPTEMBER

1984

On Wednesday I go to school and I am really dreading it. It will mean swimming and rugby and cross country. Oh no! The only source of comfort is that it'll eventually be over and it has to end by 3.30.

The 3rd year is going to be important and I know that. I will have to work hard at home and at school but the point is working at home is different because at the end of it I don't get anything. Like a computer for instance …

I've been asking for years but have I got one? All my friends knew that I was the best in the field but now I am just an ordinary person who hardly knows anything. I still want one but in a way it's too late now. I will have to start working hard and there will be no time for it. Sometimes I start crying as I think of what I've missed. I got really angry when Rupee would not let me have a good go on Pacman and if I had a computer he would ask ME to have a go but because of my dad who doesn't seem to understand that eventually computers will form the bulk of jobs and that to have a computer is going to be essential thinks £200 for a computer is not as good as spending £200 on a problem-ridden Datsun! And then my family say I don't work how can I if there's no one or thing to give me credit or a goal at the end of it?

Always I am told I am lazy, useless, inefficient ... how am I going to improve with these encouraging (ha ha) remarks? If, say, dad told me if I did well in school then I would get a Commodore then that would be an incentive, but knowing dad that has not even crossed his mind.

SUNDAY 14 JULY

1985

Live Aid yesterday. I almost went because Paul Wilson had 2 tickets going but dad wouldn't let me go. I will never ever forgive him for that and will never be the same again. I am sure. Also to add to my disgustingly bad fortunes I fell asleep a few minutes before Duran Duran were singing in Philadelphia. Queen were classic, Phil Collins and David Bowie were brilliant and so was Elton John. There is never going to be another concert ever again and I almost went. Someday, if I am a mega millionaire I will organise another Live Aid, and then I will go. Someday.

'Frankie' is number 1, 'Axel F' number 2 and 'Crazy for You' is number 3.

SATURDAY 8 MARCH
1986

Am bit depressed at state of clothes. Have worn same thing every day since September while all my friends have got different things. I wish I could buy some with my own money. Trouble is, I ain't got none!

I have been thinking about this and trying to come up with some money-making schemes. I've got an idea of a newsletter which would give hints on unit trusts, stocks and shares but the *Herald* did not want to print it.

SUNDAY 9 MARCH
1986

Steve Wright was on live from New York. Diana Ross is number one with 'Chain Reaction'. Have been reading book on positive thinking. Hope I can imagine myself to fame and fortune. Have been concerned about hair. Would like it to grow long at the back but it seems to curl up. Also I wish I could go to a real barber.

Reflecting on this diary if I become famous I'll probably get it published. That should earn me a bit. This diary is one of the few things which I really value. I mean as you go through you are turning back the pages of your mind and of time. Those days will never come back. When I read this in 1988 or whatever I'll think they were the good old days but they are not really that good you know. I have had to do without a lot of things which one may consider luxuries, but I would say would have done me a lot of good. For example a computer, and clothes, proper ones, regularly.

What really makes me really sick are those that get rich while young and with no talent. Like Samantha Fox. I mean even if I become rich it'll probably be when the money's no use to me. I will have to pass it on to my children. Lucky sods.

THURSDAY 21 — FULL MOON

good day - never again morning went round to James
gun I going to get so 24 weeks
drunk as I was last
night - so immature and shamefull - Embarrassing
+ at a party - not my own house. Anyway I've
learnt my lesson. Met Martin this afternoon
on ☐ - fountain closed. Me Kim Martin Gill +
Karen all went to the Melting Pot after being
chucked out of the monkee - The old bag
wouldn't serve us. Then just mucked around
generally in the ☐ - sat on the
grass + then looked for nail varnish
ma owes me. for my shoe repairs [30p]
Lavells - Goose (or Sheerah are going to
have a promotion bum of them
Talked to Johnny in

FRIDAY 22

this is written on
Monday so - can't remember much. I think I went
to the fountain this afternoon - oh yes of course
Martins O-levels - he got 1 his art - grade C
oh well - he was pissed + didn't really care +
neither do his ma + pa. Johnny got 2 Greg got
3 + Tim got 5. Andy - 4, Nigel 7. Don't know
anyone that got more than 7. Went to fountain
+ then onto Martins this evening - He
wanted to go to the Blue Room in B'pool. Stayed
+ Gills this evening slept on the floor but
got so in pain went in the spare room
Kim came for coffee. Didn't get to bed
properly till 4. AM. Bloody Hell.

SATURDAY 23 — JANE + gum!

Tennis Club this evening. Work this
morning - just about sacked - bloody hell. I
enjoyed the Tennis Club
but everyone was crying -
Kim is now going back
out with Jackie. Martin
got a bit pissed + violent. Me
+ Annabell stayed at Gills for
the night. Me + A had to
went outside the front door
for Gill

SUNDAY 24 — ST BARTHOLOMEW

Fountain in
afternoon + night
enjoyed myself
+ Martin was
dead nice to
me. Stayed
the night at
Janes + me
+ Gill talked
up Johnny
P. So
then we

JENNY ECLAIR

Jenny Eclair is a comedian, novelist and actor well known for her appearances in Grumpy Old Women *and* Loose Women. *Born in 1960 in Kuala Lumpur, she returned to England at the age of two and went to school in Lytham St Annes. After early appearances in* Auf Wiedersehen, Pet *and* The Bill, *Eclair started working as a stand-up and, in 1995, became the first female solo winner of the Perrier Comedy Award.*

I started keeping a diary when I was 14, which is around the age I had my first perm, started my periods and became endlessly fascinating to myself.

The following year, my sister Sara left our small northern seaside town to study law at university in London and bought me a 1975 black and gold Biba diary. This was a thing of utter coolness. She also bought me a tin of Biba baked beans which, after guzzling the beans, I rinsed out and used as a pen tidy.

Sara continued to buy me Biba diaries for the following two years, but I seem to have mislaid 1977, which is a shame as it's the year I lost my virginity, which would have made interesting reading.

What's truly shocking about my teenage self is that I have no opinions about the world outside of my own little snog bubble. There is no mention of politics, world affairs or feminism, it's just all about me, me, me, me, me.

Sorry, I was kind of appalling.

TUESDAY 21 JANUARY
1975

Jenny is 14.

Might be buying a tartan scarf off Alex for 40p – dunno whether I've got enough cash.

THURSDAY 23 JANUARY
1975

Another day off school, ill. Ma bought me a *Look In* to read. After school Jane and Gill came to see me, to tell me the news. There was none.

MONDAY 27 JANUARY
1975

Another day off school, Gill came round to see me after school, Rick didn't ring last night but his friends told her that he said he's finished with her, so she told them to tell him she'd beaten him to it, so we're both fancy free on Saturday and if we've got the money we're going to get drunk.

SATURDAY 1 FEBRUARY

1975

Tonight was dead good. Cricket Club (dance). I was with Martin for about 2 hours from 9 o'clock onwards – he's really nice. All warm. And when I remember being with him, I tie it up with Rod Stewart's 'Maggie May' and Dave Bowie's 'Gene Genie' [*The Jean Genie*]. When Martin went to the bog, I could have gone with Rick Webb and Mal. Wish I had gone with Mal – Martin wouldn't have minded. He's so sweet and goes a bit.

TUESDAY 11 FEBRUARY

1975

Pancake Tuesday, had about four. Ace.

SUNDAY 9 MARCH

1975

Mothering Sunday – bought the old toad some Matchmakers. 25p.

FRIDAY 9 MAY

1975

Martin came back to my house for a coffee and we had a nice time even though Mum and Dad were in.

SATURDAY 10 MAY

1975

Martin was in a great mood, then this evening we went to the Albany – you had to be 18! Had a great time, except I had to be home by 11.30. Martin got a request played for me 'Sugar Pie Honey' and the DJ said, 'this is specially for Jenny who can now show us how to dance'. See, I had my green circular velvet skirt on and was having a good bop and everyone really enjoyed themselves and on the way home Martin came in for coffee and said, 'I couldn't do without you.'

MONDAY 14 JULY

1975

I rang Martin and we argued quite badly and then he put the phone down. Jane came round and we went and got some crisps.

THURSDAY 7 AUGUST

1975

Gill came for lunch. Had all this drink, went to the square, was a bitch to Martin and now regret it, told him I'd thought of finishing. Went to Gill's for tea and watched *TOTP* which was a bit crap. Then went home and read all about Oral Sex.

FRIDAY 22 AUGUST
1975

Martin got his O-level results – got one C in Art – oh well.

TUESDAY 26 AUGUST
1975

Noel Edmunds is fit.

FRIDAY 29 AUGUST
1975

This afternoon I finished with Martin at 3.00 in the fountain. I just gave him back his ring and could hardly speak and just cried and cried all afternoon in the fountain – he didn't seem to give a damn. Not 2 shits and then everything seemed worthless, the whole five and 3/4 months.

MONDAY 10 JANUARY
1976

At school, Jane trimmed my hair and we made eyes at the window cleaners – one of which was rather fit. Steven rang twice tonight, I hope to God he passes his driving test tomorrow, he'll be so disappointed if he doesn't and I'll be so annoyed because if he gets it he can take me all over the place, like the Mardi Gras in Blackpool.

THURSDAY 3 FEBRUARY

1976

Steven failed his driving test, which is a drag, putting him in a foul mood.

Went to a jumble sale got some Levi's for an incredible £1 when they sell in the shops for £11 – and they fit.

THURSDAY 10 FEBRUARY

1976

I am going to be famous. I have just realised that I can't not be, if I am going to be happy.

WEDNESDAY 30 MARCH

1976

Great day, was very nervous all afternoon, couldn't concentrate in triple art. Tonight was great, such fun, best thing was Mr Ellison saying that I was a natural, that some had it and some didn't and I had and that I'd risen to the occasion.

FRIDAY 1 APRIL

1976

Last night was great, the play went excellently and the after party at the tennis club was great fun. I had to be controlled. Felt so good I wanted to take my clothes off.

MONDAY 16 MAY

1976

Ma's birthday, I do like her, I bought her some Tweed perfume. Nanna came for tea – pears stuffed with prawns coated in cream cheese and cream with lettuce, pork in wine and a red sauce and cherry gateau.

If I live this far it will be my 17th
birthday. Gosh!

Not much of a birthday really
which is always disappointing.
Felt ill. £20 from mum
£4 W.H. Smith vouchers from
Ann + Dave.
Bought meself track-suit, bit
small tho' not to worry.

Walking up windmill hill topless
woman sunbathing, her paper (a graph
or summit) blew away, being a perfect
gentleman (!) I retrieved it for her,
~~could slip to too to yeah~~ but only
cos I was a bit too slow to realise
that if I didn't get it she would
have to have got up to retrieve it
herself. Damn!

Lots of riots around country
now, at first a manifestation of
discontent + frustration, but where will 't
lead? I ponder.

ROB NEWMAN

Rob Newman is a comedian and writer, who shot to fame in the 1990s as part of The Mary Whitehouse Experience *and* Newman and Baddiel, *with his erstwhile comedy partner David Baddiel. Newman now works as a solo writer, performer and political activist. He was born in 1964.*

Reading my diary now, I don't know why I wasn't panicking more. I apply to five universities, only to be turned down by them all. I should panic. Nowadays I panic at much less. Was I simply too pre-occupied with separating my monobrow by using Jolen bleach and tweezers? Or was my lack of panic – as I suspect – nothing to do with me at all, but more to do with the world in which I was keeping a diary?

I wonder if it came from the fact that my generation enjoyed a broad and bouncy safety net, making us sanguine about the future. We were sure that living standards would improve for everyone, sure our lives would be an improvement on our parents' lives, sure that the ratio of state to private school intake at universities would continue to tilt in our favour. Back in 1981 progress towards ever-increasing social equality seemed a law of nature, as inevitable as bumping into Joe Strummer every time I went to London. (Which now reads as totally bizarre!)

When I did at last find a university that would accept me – Cambridge – I was eligible for a full maintenance grant. Many tens of thousands of us routinely received that full grant and the consequences were immense. Tuition? Free. Accommodation? Free. Plus a generous living allowance (supplemented in my case by a hardship grant from Philadelphia, USA – which I spent on black suede pointy shoes, regrettable flowery shirts and weekly entry to Ronelles disco).

Looking back from the twenty-first century, the notion of free university education as a universal right seems like something from a dream, as do all the diary entries recording yet another chance encounter with the Clash front man. But they happened. They really happened. And one of them could happen again.

THURSDAY 29 JANUARY

1981

Rob is 16.

Went to London to buy jacket but all about £90–100! Bought wonderful huge black jumper £15 in Kensington Market.

Only did one cool thing all day. Girl (new-wave-ish) got on the bus and we exchanged glances from a few seats away on top deck, and smiled a bit. And then she overheard when I was cornered by 3 middle-aged Yanks who sat where I was and said: 'We're from Texas … Would you like to visit the States?'

Me: 'I'd like to visit Russia.'
'Why?' etc.
Me: 'Seems like a nice place …'
echoed by Yank: 'Seems like a nice place.'
Me: ' … strong ideological spine.'

This shut 'em up until girl got off at Baker Street. Then, seeing my gaze following her, Yank tapped me on the knee.

'Never mind, you'll find one like her in Russia.' And started chatting again.

WEDNESDAY 29 APRIL

1981

Did paper round then remembered I'd forgot flipping front door key so would have had to sit on doorstep until mum came home at 2.30.

At some point in the not too distant future they'll find out I tried (stupidly) to break in and left a chunk out of the window frame; consequently I will have my features rearranged.

Made five big mistakes:

Forgetting key
trying to break in
not stopping mum in car
forgetting book
and one other – can't remember what though!

THURSDAY 30 APRIL
1981

Sixth mistake apparent. I left garden shears on step. Now they're *looking* for what I might have used them for and actually mentioned 'housebreaking'. Therefore, my friend, it is *certain* I feel that at any time now there will be a fatalistic knock at the door or a sudden storming in. 'We are the dead.'

Sold bike for £2.50! (tee-hee)

FRIDAY 8 MAY
1981

Had series of bollockings (three) over pissing about in German, argued with one teacher, ignored other two. Must be perfect from now on in German. Letter being sent to mum, must intercept it. I'm wasting intelligence.

Alternative Comedy module on TV. Quite good.

TUESDAY 7 JULY

1981

If I live this far it will be my 17th birthday. Gosh!

Not much of a birthday really, which is always disappointing. Felt ill. Got £20 from mum and £4 WHSmith vouchers from Ann and Dave. Bought myself track suit, bit small.

Walking up Windmill Hill, topless woman sunbathing, her paper (a *Telegraph* or summat) blew away, being a perfect gentleman (!) I retrieved it for her, but only cos I was a bit too slow to realise that if I didn't get it she would have to have got up to retrieve it herself. Damn!

Lots of riots around the country now, at first a manifestation of discontent and frustration, but where will it lead? I ponder.

THURSDAY 9 JULY

1981

Rumours of race riots etc. coming to Hitchin, don't know whether to fight on the side of the blacks and Asians or just stay at home and keep out of it ... anyway, called local fascist, Logan, a 'wanker' to his face on Hermitage Road with Yoyo. But on me own. Quite brave of me, I thought. What a wonderful character I am, eh? Gimme a medal!

Trouble at home again, door off hinges, violence, room, etc.

Put all money in bank as emergency measure to avoid threatened taking of money for keep. If necessary I will 'lose' bank book.

THURSDAY 22 OCTOBER
1981

Go to see The Clash (at last). Me last fling.

Went with John, train to Charing Cross, went in Wellington pub. Gig was really good, audience quite cool too. Stayed on balcony for Talisman's brilliant set and beginning of Clash's then went down and pogoed. Clash opened with wailing of sirens, then border-crossing barriers with a green light on 'em – came down, slowly, then the Clash. Even the stuff from *Sandanista* and *London Calling* sounded good and pacey. Set included 'Clash City Rockers', 'Complete Control', 'White Man', 'Janie Jones', 'Career Opportunities', 'Safe European Home', 'London Calling'.

John said at King's Cross 'Did you write a thesis on Clash lyrics once?'

'Yeah,' I said, not wishing to undo any budding legendary status.

'Cor, you didn't tell me about it.'

Had Wimpy before and after gig. Got home around 3am.

FRIDAY 23 OCTOBER
1981

Did paper round about 10.00am. Went bed again till about 12.45. Poked eye with tweezer, very painful. Looked cool today in school, 'after' look and seasoned veteran punk. Wore red braces, and hair a bit lank, eyes, face. Goodge said 'You look ill Rob.' Great!

Got to school 1.45. Apparently, Digger read out my Chaucer translation (magic!) and had a go at Hartson for his being so crap. Yea-hey!

SATURDAY 24 OCTOBER
1981

Went CND rally in Hyde Park. SAW JOE STRUMMER yet again, spoke to him about gig etc. but dried up and inarticulate.

Met Rachel, Becky and Vanessa – punkettes from Welwyn Garden City.

Spoke to Tony Benn and made him laugh/smile upon 'I hope you aren't misquoted by the time it gets to the States after CBS interview'. Surely a photo containing me must appear somewhere. Saw Michael Foot from a long distance.

Sid and people actually being nice to me – like when I stopped in tube station to read *NME*, Sid came back to look for me. Saw quite a few beautiful girls, everyone a heartbreaker. CND rally preaching to the converted really, too much to say about it here. BECAME FRIENDS WITH THIS JULIE STONE girl doing photography at Bristol College. Met her in romantic situation of asking her the way to Battersea Park, whilst upon Bridge near Festival Hall, slightly foggy evening. Chatting, then helped her carry bag and both got on the same bus, here to see her parents in Digswell, then she took off her hat and she was really beautiful. Sat next to her on coach home. She took photos of little girl sitting in front of us. Had Farley's Rusks. Walked home in pissing rain.

THURSDAY 31 DECEMBER

1981

Good day this.

About 4 o'clock left to go to Sid's but only me and Ada. Went Sid's for half an hour then popped over Ada's, sat in Viv's downstairs room. Had mince pies and half of Ada and Viv's dinners. Viv told Ada that she wants to go out with me. Oh dear. Returned to Sid's.

Sid nipped out for legendary 'quick half, I'll be straight back' so after a while we went over to the Plume of Feathers and found him pissed as a newt in his pyjama top. Fancy dress over at Plume. Kim girl as French waitress. Poor Debbie as Hilda Ogden: about 20 persons said 'You should have dressed up.' Prideaux as Dracula. Adi as Flasher. Paula as ballerina. Sid as a very drunk man in his pyjama top.

French waitress Kim put rouge under my cheekbones. Missed my cue with her by about 5 seconds. Got 2 kisses off her at midnight though. Found her plastic red rose which I kept. Kisses and handshakes all round. Buck's Head and home. Sid in a state. Story continues January 1st of 1982 diary. (Sounds as if I'm a 'partygoer' dancing and revelling from pub to pub, diary to diary! But this is probably the only New Year's Eve I've not spent alone for a long time.)

Monday 7th August 1978

It was raining again when I got up and Mummy had already started to clean up the house for the Williams' return in the evening. Unfortunately, Mummy had left the sitting-room window open and some of the cats kept coming in. There are three cats: a ginger one, Tommy, a black and white one, Pusskins who has adopted them and a black one who is nothing to do with them at all. Nevertheless the first two mentioned are fed by the Williams' although Elizabeth was entrusted with that job, whilst they were away – which she took quite seriously.

At 11.30 we went into Keswick, lunched and did shopping for essentials such as bread and looked around in some beautiful book shops such as 'The Silk Purse'. On the way home we went down to the Pencil Factory to see if it was open for inspection since Mummy wanted to look – unfortunately it was not.

KATE MOSSE

Kate Mosse is an international best-selling novelist, non fiction author, essayist and playwright. Her historical novels include Labyrinth *and* The Burning Chambers, *the first in a sequence of novels set against the backdrop of the French Wars of Religion. The Founder Director of the Women's Prize for Fiction, Mosse is Deputy Chair of the National Theatre and hosts the pre- and post-interview series at Chichester Festival Theatre. She divides her time between Carcassonne and Chichester, where she was born in 1961.*

I never was a teenager who wrote a diary. But, for two weeks in the summer of 1978, I filled an old green hardback notebook with a day-to-day account of a family holiday in the Lake District for my grandmother. Pussy Cat Granny was in her late seventies and very ill. When she discovered my parents, two sisters and I were going to Newlands Valley for a fortnight – a place where she'd spent many happy childhood holidays in the 1890s and 1900s and where, in time, she had taken her own children – she asked me to keep a record of the holiday: the brook, Stair Mill, Borrowdale, Catbells, the Bowder Stone and Causey Pike. I had a boyfriend, puffed on the occasional cigarette and drank cheap cider when I thought I could get away with it (small-town life in Chichester in the late 1970s), but for the diary I adopted a peculiar old-fashioned voice. (I was going for Jane Austen penmanship, but it came out as a cross between Enid Blyton and Milly-Molly-Mandy.) I tried to write how I thought she would want me to write and to pick out places and people she would remember. I even stuck in a few maps and postcards.

The result? You can see for yourself. It's really awful – sanctimonious, prim, faux formal and dull! So very, very dull. There's A LOT of information about the road traffic system (between Sussex and the Lake District), endless descriptions of the weather (wet and windy) and of family outings that didn't quite come off (the Pencil Factory was closed). My sisters – now also in their fifties – still remind me of how I referred to them throughout as 'the children'. It certainly doesn't suggest I might earn my living by spinning stories. Talent, there is none. And yet …

When I remember reading it aloud to my grandmother in the last weeks of her life in September 1978, remember how she listened and smiled and imagined herself back in her beloved Lake District, it might just be one of the most important things I ever wrote.

SUNDAY 30 JULY

1978

Kate is 16.

Everyone was, theoretically, supposed to be up early but, as is usually the case, in practice we were not. We were all given instructions on how and what to pack. Surprisingly, Caroline and Elizabeth were conveniently out of view when they should have been packing, but they finished before I did since I could not decide what to wear or to take with me.

Since Mummy had told us that we would probably be having fewer 'proper' homemade meals, she cooked us a superb roast beef lunch which rendered everyone too 'fat' and lazy to be doing anything.

I was shown Daddy's map routes since I was to be the navigator. Following this, all the now completed cases were placed in the hall.

Daddy and I bedded down early since, for us, Monday was going to be a long day. I simply thought about my new navigationary job, which proved to be interesting at the very least.

MONDAY 31 JULY

1978

Monday came, having no alternative, and I was awoken by the not-so-gentle patter of rain on my window followed, very soon after, with flashes of sheet lightning and rather huge thunder groans which, luckily, does not scare me in the slightest. I found these weather conditions quite extraordinary since the weather charts had foretold sun and showers down here as opposed to rain and showers in the Lakes: since *we* already seemed to be experiencing a deluge I did seriously wonder if we would still have a destination to arrive at by the evening. It all adds to the excitement though ... I think!

We set off at 10am exactly and it was still pouring very heavily indeed. Due to the appalling weather conditions and getting lost in Newbury we arrived in Banbury at 1pm in time for lunch. As we were returning from lunch we saw a yellow Cortina drive into a blue van right at the actual 'Banbury Cross'.

We hit the motorway at 2.45pm and it was still raining. The journey was long and at Spaghetti Junction there was, or rather had been, another accident. We stopped for a coffee at Keele between junctions 15 and 16. We then travelled straight on stopping only at Forton (junction 33) for a quick breath of fresh air.

There were many interesting sights. Just before junction 26 there was an old, now un-used, cotton mill. By junction 34 was the university of Lancaster which looked incredibly space-like. By junction 38, near to Shaps Fell, I saw, for the first time, those beautiful little stone walls peculiar to the Lakes, and just after we saw a cow using a bridge crossing over us – which seemed rather strange.

We finally left the motorway and travelled towards Keswick – the beautiful view being rather spoiled by the rain and clouds so I could see very little, in fact.

The drive into Stair and the mill were beautiful. We had a cup of tea and rang Mummy and then unpacked – I am in the room to the left at the top of the stairs. It's all really lovely and P.S. Granny, my Dorothy Wordsworth book is on my bedside table.

WEDNESDAY 2 AUGUST

1978

It was a lovely sunny day so I got up early (awoken by the sun since my room faces east), laid breakfast and then took Mummy and Daddy a cup of tea. Breakfast was over quickly and we were out on 'Stoney Croft' bridge by 9.40am. We explored and climbed for two and a half hours during which time we went to 'Spider Wells', which is really lovely. I climbed around there and found a beautiful, quite large, pool and sat by it for ages just looking into it – it is so nice, I can see why you especially liked it.

At about 2.15, we went into Keswick for a quick look around. Daddy joined the AA.

But we returned to Keswick twice after we had left it since Elizabeth decided she would like a walking stick. Then coming out again I saw a pencil shop and we all had to go back to look at it.

Finally we arrived home and after tea we all walked up to the beck with our new walking sticks.

After dinner we sat with a fire and wrote letters and postcards to everyone. We bedded down early since due to our strenuous day we were all very, very tired; it had been a most agreeable and enjoyable day.

SUNDAY 6 AUGUST

1978

It was pouring down with rain when we got up and departed for church. Once there, the lovely old church-cum-school struck everyone as particularly nice. Daddy read the lesson from a beautiful old Bible on the stand, and it was pleasant to use the old service as opposed to the Series 3 employed at Fishbourne Church. The sermon was very good and afterwards Mrs Standing showed me the Bible you had donated, whilst Elizabeth made friends and conversed with Mrs Potts who seemed quite charming.

In the afternoon, although still pouring down at intervals, we took courage in hand and decided to climb Catbells which we did completely, there and back, in two hours exactly. We did not stay long at the summit since a mist was falling but the sun came out while we were on the ridge and the view was really lovely.

After supper a policewoman came to the door and asked Daddy if we had seen a young girl around, since she had not returned from a walk five hours ago. Later, Daddy went out to look for her and was gone so long that we were all just coming out of the gate to look for him when he re-appeared. The evening seemed to be blessed with strange occurrences, for at a half past a gentleman came to the door and asked if Daddy would help to extricate a cow from a barbed wire fence in the field beside the mill. They finally succeeded in doing this and Daddy returned exhausted and therefore we all then went to bed, tired by the day's work and exertions. Upstairs Daddy said that the Warden, who had been helping to pull the cow out, had had a very busy day and before coming to Stair had rescued two young boys climbing up the quarry face near to the Bowder Stone. He said that he was cross since it is marked as dangerous, it was slippery due to the rain and night was falling. The poor Warden had spent a very busy evening – just like Daddy!

MONDAY 7 AUGUST

1978

It was raining again when I got up. At 11.30 we went into Keswick, lunched and did shopping for essentials such as bread and looked around some beautiful bookshops such as 'The Silk Purse'. On the way home we went down to the Pencil Factory to see if it was open for inspection since Mummy wanted to look – unfortunately it was not.

THURSDAY 10 AUGUST

1978

It was sunny but it seemed rather sad that the weather was brightening up just when we were about to go.

We went into Keswick for a last look around and we bought any things we had had our eyes on.

We had to pack, so much of Thursday afternoon was spent packing and taking a last look at the beck.

We had a cooked meal since it would be our last proper meal for a day.

We did not play cards since Daddy thought it imperative that we should have a good night – which we did.

FRIDAY 11 AUGUST

1978

We loaded up and after we had put Mummy and the two children on the 9.59 train from Penrith, it seemed remarkable that within 8½ hours we would be 350 miles away: but we were. Our holiday was over!

more even after a small
meal eg

and that   his wing
feathers are   drooping

Tuesday 2nd November 1975.
He weighed 4.75 but he ate
well all day and he spent from
6.30 t indoors Before tea he
weighed 5.75 and he ate all
of his tea although hee did not
eat it all at 6.00.
Wednesday 3rd November 1975.
He seemed better at 3.00 am
and at 12.00 he had a lot of
rhubarb infusion with egg yolk
and this made him a lot happier
and turned his mutes blacker

CHRIS PACKHAM

Chris Packham is a pioneering naturalist, writer and broadcaster. Born in 1961, he became famous for presenting The Really Wild Show, *and since 2009 has presented* Springwatch, Autumnwatch *and* Winterwatch. *Packham is a vocal campaigner for wildlife conservation, a vegetarian, and has spoken publicly about his diagnosis with Asperger's syndrome.*

Harriet Jaine, producer of My Teenage Diary: Chris Packham's diaries are unlike any others we've featured on *My Teenage Diary*. All teenage diaries are different, but they generally share similar concerns – sex, school, family life, rock and roll and, of course, some soul searching. But Chris's diaries are about nature. From 27 March 1975 he began to keep detailed notes of his animal sightings in diary form, and these provide a fascinating record of the young naturalist learning his craft. From his capture of a grass snake to his observations of two shrews, in this diary the young Chris Packham is learning how to document, observe and talk about the natural world.

But this catalogue of birds' nests, calls and animal remains is not devoid of human feeling – far from it. When Chris takes a young kestrel chick from its nest, begins to rear it at home and teach it to fly from the fist, his emotional life becomes inextricably tied up with the life of the bird. He recalls, 'The connection was so complete that, at that time, really nothing else existed in the world.' The detail and clarity with which he describes the bird's appetite and behaviour in the days before its death is heart-breaking. As Chris said, 'the impact of that loss has shaped the whole of my life'. Hearing Chris read aloud from this diary was an unforgettable experience – the power of the natural world to inspire and delight the human soul was clear in every word he read.

THURSDAY 27 MARCH

1975

Chris is 13.

I have decided that my natural history knowledge must be on paper because I will undoubtedly forget the chaffinch nest in my school (April '73). It will take quite a while to catch up two years of serious bird watching, and generally watching nature, so I will begin with the real start.

On a February day in 1973 I went to John Davis's house after school and brought starling, robin and dunnocks' eggs. From now on I was addicted to egg collecting.

After keeping these I was informed while replacing the front door that Nigel Barnard had found 3 red eggs and 4 blue and black spotted eggs at the school. I went with him and he showed me them.

THURSDAY 10 APRIL

1975

I went to Lower Lipham to see the kestrel but only saw it on the way back. Soon two were playing together.

I went up the airport to the old buildings. I found a mistle thrush nest and collected lots of kestrel pellets. Found a young rabbit's head (freshly eaten) and intestines.

SUNDAY 27 APRIL

1975

Went to the towpath near the weir and in the fields at the back we found a LAPWING!!! It had four warm eggs in it, and they were all pointing inwards. Two photos were taken and the lapwing made a strange call, not normal.

The kestrel was heard several times and pheasants were heard very close by. Bank voles were common.

FRIDAY 6 JUNE

1975

I found it! I watched the male fly over me and into the tree and I heard the eyasses screaming. I sat under a hawthorn and watched at first three birds. But then the male moved and made a teeet teeet sound, on which the female left the post she was sat on and with the male circled the tree until she flipped on her back and the male dropped food to her which she took to the nest and tore up for the chicks. This happened several times and each time the female returned to the nest and then to the post where she sat. Also, she had a bath in a drainage ditch while waiting for the male.

When I climbed to the nest six eyasses all looked at me with open mouth and eyes from one old crow's nest. Only a few droppings were on the ground and no pellets. It was quite a hard climb on a thin branch.

SATURDAY 14 JUNE

1975

I went to the nest in the morning and watched the male feed the chicks, one of which was a brancher. Then I checked – yes, there were six eyasses, one of which was ready.

We went back in the afternoon (with dad) who took 2 photos. I went up right to the nest and the chicks, and bundled over to the far side. I grabbed the one I wanted while only one other screamed. I put him in the ARP bag and transported him back to the car where he was put into a hessian lined box.

When we arrived home he was jessed and belled easily and then put on a perch. He ate after 5 minutes and I fed him stewing beef and waked him until 8 o'clock Sunday morning when we both slept. He did not bate much until early morning and early afternoon. He resents the jesses and bells and being put onto the perch. He is in good condition and only bates when hungry.

During the night he produced a well formed pellet after several efforts.

He eats easily and has not got much down. He lets me touch him and was introduced to daylight at 11.00 on Sunday morning. I am writing this on Sunday afternoon.

SUNDAY 15 JUNE

1975

After 12.00 noon we introduced him slowly to the light by opening the door and curtains. He did not bate very much and ate well. I introduced him to the television set and he appeared all right and bated occasionally. He slept in my room and was all right.

AUGUST
1975

Eventually he landed on my head. I cast him up again and he immediately chased a sparrow over the field and then hung around until landing in a small tree. When I called him down he tried to land in the trees to the left and on failing there he flew right over to the large oak near Adrian's house and circled three times here trying to land in the tree. Enough. I brought him home after he bated twice from the fist.

TUESDAY 2 NOVEMBER
1975

He weighed 4.75 but he ate well all day and he spent from 6.30 indoors. Before tea he weighed 5.75 and he ate all of his tea.

WEDNESDAY 3 NOVEMBER
1975

He seemed better at 3.00 am and at 12.00 he had a lot of rhubarb infusion with egg yolk and this made him a lot happier and turned his mutes blacker.

THURSDAY 4 NOVEMBER
1975

He weighed 4.5 oz and he ate well at dinner and breakfast. I gave him the rhubarb infusion at 12.00 and at tea time he ate well but did not finish his meal. He was not digesting at all so I will get up at 3.00 am and feed him some more.

FRIDAY 5 DECEMBER
1975

I dosed him with kaolin and glucose solution at 6.00 and 9.00 after a day of very low weight. We took him to the local vet.

SATURDAY 6 DECEMBER
1975

He had kaolin, glucose and Penbritin but did not eat all day. He died at 6.30pm.

MONDAY 29 DECEMBER
1975

As I may have written in this book, Kes was actually cured after his first dose of Penbritin. But as I said to the vet his droppings were still bad. If I had known what symptoms diarrhoea had, he could have quite easily have been saved with Kaolin at this early date. A missing scrap of knowledge was very costly.

TUESDAY 30 DECEMBER
1975

Maybe if I had brought him indoors before I did during the cold week, he would have lived, an unforgiveable mistake.

SUNDAY 13 JUNE
1976

At 1.30pm today at Studland just past the first car park out in a dried salt marsh I caught my first smooth snake. It was a very large specimen – 62.5cm. It was very violent on being caught, dribbling and snapping and in no way feigning death. He has just eaten and is very rounded and purple underneath.

THURSDAY 29 JUNE
1976

I let the smooth snake go at Studland Heath.

THURSDAY 29 JULY

1976

At 11.30am this morning I was bitten for the first time by a grass snake. It was caught on Tuesday 27th by Nigel Barnard at Black Dyke near Highbridge. It was caught at 1.00pm and it struggled violently and smelt. It is a large (3ft) specimen and as I picked it up it struggled and bit me between forefinger and thumb. Then with gloves on I approached it on the tank floor and it exploded and struck out like an adder completely covering my finger with its mouth. Only a small incision was made.

WEDNESDAY 19 OCTOBER

1977

I have in my possession the British Record Female Smooth Newt. It is 100mm+ long and the biggest before by Smith is 97mm. I got it from Sarah Osman's who lives at the top of the hill, but I understand it came from a pond in Norris Hill.

THURSDAY 8 DECEMBER

1977

THE COMMON SHREWS: I have now had 'Sniff' since Tuesday week and he had not had any drinking water at all and he had been eating casters, beet, corn, woodlice and worms and he is very well and active both day and night, constantly 'surfacing' above the leaves and wafting his nose about. His eyesight is very poor, limited to about 8cms and his sense of smell does not extend much further. When I put him with 'Scrum' (who was caught last Saturday, was violent and died this afternoon) he was the weaker of the two and ran off squeaking. It was interesting to see that in the small box where they were they constantly marked by rubbing their side against in the corners and the food which was put in for them. Actual biting and tussling only occurred twice in about 22 encounters and a wide range of notes were produced. I gave 'Scrum' to the bird at 6.00pm today.

And now Chris's final diary entry as a teenager …

SATURDAY 17 JANUARY
1981

I went with Pete and Joanne to Pagham Harbour and we had a brilliant day. Firstly we saw a FLAMINGO in ferry pond. It was right in the middle feeding away and sniffing about. It was fully adult and a bright orangey pink. BUT the best bird for ages was a HENHARRIER female which flew across a beautiful sunrise over Church Norton Harbour. It approached right in front of us and flapped about over the field to be chased by crows. It eventually ended up being the chaser, before it kept disappearing in its lazy flappy flight. It was simply superb and fulfilled classic Harrier poses and was in good condition …

Mick Jagger. And the tension grew and grew throughout the performance as group after weedy group came and left the stage. And then, my goodness, it was time for the Rolling Stones to appear. I felt so excited and wide-eyed & trembling, and then the curtains drew on the darkened stage. I clutched my binoculars and was almost crying. One of those dark figures that one could not yet properly see was Mick Jagger. And then the stage grew lighter and I saw him! I don't know whether I screamed or cried or what. I could see him so large and clear through the binoculars that he looked right next to me. I could see every check of his blue criss-cross shirt. I felt very like crying, not screaming, the whole way through it. I always wondered what I would do if one did not know that lots of girls screamed or else cried, what would feel natural, and crying did. Not crying just with sadness & frustration but with happiness and sadness too. There was a lot of screaming down in the stalls, as a background, so you couldn't hear all that well, though better than I'd imagined. But just seeing was so lovely. Mick was absolutely super. I loved the way he took off his jacket &

JULIA DONALDSON

*Julia Donaldson, who was born Julia Shields
in London in 1948, is a prolific children's
poet and performer, and a former Children's
Laureate. Her classic* The Gruffalo *is one of the
most popular children's books ever published.
Donaldson received an* MBE *in 2011.*

I kept a diary from when I was 11 and still buying doll's-house
furniture with my pocket money until I was 18, awaiting
A-level results and nurturing a passion for a French art
student.

I was a London girl but always keen on nature and the
countryside, so in some of the entries I am meeting a friend
'under Eros' for coffee in a nearby Wimpy bar, while in others
I am off youth-hostelling, waxing lyrical about footpaths and
stiles and bemoaning the drippiness of hairy-legged hikers.

It was the Swinging Sixties but I went to an all-girls'
school so it was quite hard to meet boys, except at dances
where you were either a wallflower or else trying to escape
the clutches of some over-ardent stranger. In my dreams life

was very different: I would bump into Mick Jagger in Carnaby Street and he would fall instantly in love with me.

Re-reading the diaries has brought a mixture of pleasure and pain. But mostly I feel an affection for my younger self, and don't think I've changed all that much. I still have similar moods, triumphs and despair, worries and regrets. And I'm glad to say I have got over Mick Jagger.

SUNDAY 1 AUGUST
1965

Julia is 16.

When we got out of the tube the road was filled with teenagers
and policemen. Yes, this was the London Palladium (where
the best group in the world were going to be playing), and a
discouraging sight it was. When we reached the stage door
there were hundreds of girls there. Everyone had autograph
books, and their highest hope was to send them in for
autographs, or to touch the sleeve of even the feeblest member
of the band. But Chris's and my aim was … to TALK WITH
MICK JAGGER IN HIS DRESSING ROOM!

It was near the end of the first performance and we could
hear the Rolling Stones playing through the walls. Then a
car drew up and some official-looking men carried bottles
of coke and trays of fish and chips for the Rolling Stones.
Presently people began to pour out of the theatre – the first
performance had ended. Some girls were crying hysterically,
frustrated instead of satisfied by seeing their idols, and a few
of them were lying down on some steps in tears. Suddenly
there was a shriek from one of the girls. 'Billy!' She had faintly
seen Bill Wyman in an upstairs window. Bill Wyman is about
the least alluring of the Stones but at once piercing screams
rent the air. Everyone screeched, 'Billy, Billy!' and ran wild.
The horrible smug hard policemen had to keep people back.
And there was a horrible policewoman with black stuff on her
eyelids.

I began to feel rather depressed. So *many* people loved the
Rolling Stones, especially Mick Jagger, who really is rather

super, and in a way it was horrible to be one of thousands of stupid clamouring fans. We almost decided to go, as our little story of how Mick Jagger had said I could bring Chris along seemed so feeble.

But in the end I went up to a doorkeeper-like man and told him that I'd talked to Mick Jagger in Hampstead and that he'd said I could bring Chris if they were playing in London in the summer. All of the official men went serious and quite sympathetic, and to our great surprise they consulted each other and said I could write down who I was and my message, and they'd see what could be done. So, feeling very excited and with my hands and knees shaking, I wrote a note to Mick Jagger.

Everyone seemed to believe our story, or at least admire our pluck for making it up, and lots of girls asked where we met Mick Jagger. Then a hardened-looking fair-haired man in a checked shirt came back with the note. At first he said it would be no good, but then he became more interested and asked when I'd met Mick Jagger and what my name was. Chris had her passport with her to show she was German, as if that proved everything.

Suddenly the fair-haired man looked decisive and said, 'OK I'll take your note along to them.' Gosh, we were so excited! The second performance had already begun, but the Rolling Stones were to appear last, and we could hear Mick Jagger practising the mouth organ in a basement room. Then there was a break in the playing – he must be reading the note now! The playing started again and we waited to hear the result of it all.

At last our man returned. 'He says he remembers you but he's afraid you can't come now,' was the message. Fancy Mick

Jagger's saying that when I've never really met him! (Except in my dreams.) We were so sad because we'd come so near to seeing him but not quite managed it. However, there are two consolations. The first one is that we had a much more exciting time than if we'd just waited and said nothing, like most of the other girls. I was so surprised that they weren't all trying to get in by subtle methods. The second is that I've come into contact with Mick Jagger, and he's even read my writing!

SATURDAY 25 SEPTEMBER
1965

At last I have seen him. At last I have seen Mick Jagger. Geraldine and I went to see the Rolling Stones' show yesterday ... The tension grew and grew as group after weedy group came and left the stage. And then, my goodness, it was time for the Rolling Stones to appear ... The curtains drew on the darkened stage. I clutched my binoculars and was almost crying. One of those dark figures that one could not yet properly see was Mick Jagger. And then the stage grew lighter and I *saw* him! I could see him so large and clear through the binoculars that he looked right next to me. I could see every check of his blue criss-cross shirt ... There was a lot of screaming down in the stalls, as a background, so you couldn't hear all that well ... but just seeing was so lovely. Mick was absolutely super. I loved the way he took off his jacket and flung it down after the first song, and pushed his sleeves up a bit, and for some reason I loved it when he once or twice tickled his chest.

SATURDAY 9 OCTOBER

1965

I just *must* meet him soon ... I'm going to try every method.
I shall ask everyone I know if they know anyone who knows
him. I'll find out his address somehow (perhaps from the
list of voters, or by ringing all the Jaggers in the telephone
directory and seeing if they're related to him). But the main
method, thought up by Sylvia's mother, is brilliant. When I
find his address I shall go round there with a questionnaire
from the Market Research thing, which Sylvia's mother knows
all about. I'll go to a few houses first and then go there, and
say I'm going to every tenth house and is there anyone there
between the ages of eighteen and twenty-five. There is? Well,
what profession? Musician? Oh yes, that's on our list. Oh!
If only it should work! He would answer all the questions,
quite personal ones, and we'd laugh together about how silly
some of them are. And he'd just have to like me. I am quite
determined, and determination can do anything. I had yet
another dream, my sixth, about him the other night.

FRIDAY 22 OCTOBER

1965

Bubbles of excitement are bubbling about inside me. Yes, I
am one step nearer to Mick Jagger. Geraldine looked up the
addresses of Jaggers near Dartford, where I know Mick's
parents live. I phoned the most likely one and asked for Chris

(Mick's brother) to find out if it was the right address. And the pleasant-voiced woman said he'd gone out ten minutes ago!!!! That means that it *must* be his parents' house.

MONDAY 25 OCTOBER

1965

All those bubbles of excitement have been cruelly burst. I rang up the Jaggers today and said, 'Is Mick there?' 'No.' She sounded a bit snappy today. 'Well, do you think you could possibly give me his address?' 'No, I'm afraid not.' I told my deceitful story about having borrowed two LPs when Mick lived in Hampstead and not knowing his new address. Mrs Jagger was terribly nice. She wasn't at all snappy any more and she kept making suggestions about how I could send them to their manager or record company, or even to them. No, Mike (as she called him) wasn't there, and of course he was going to America on Wednesday. She didn't know if she even knew his address offhand, but anyway she wasn't allowed to divulge it because of all the fans. (She laughed rather apologetically but sounded firm about it.) Well, she would tell Mike I'd rung about the LPs (I said I was called Jackie – I couldn't say Julia because I'd told her I was called Julia on Friday, that happy day when I asked for Chris Jagger). She was very nice and we chatted politely but all the time I felt an awful dull feeling inside, and when I put the receiver down I burst into tears.

SATURDAY 9 JANUARY

1966

Geraldine and I dolled ourselves up excitedly, and I experimented with the eye make-up which I had bought in Woolworth's on the way to my piano lesson. We arrived at the party at about 8, and before long people were streaming in until it was so squashed you could hardly move an inch. I felt very awkward and nervous, tagging on to Geraldine. When she was asked to dance I felt awful, and wandered around searching for crisps, tears pricking my eyes. However soon a chunky fair-haired boy asked me to dance. I felt that he had just taken pity on me and was being a bit condescending, but he was very sexy, and knew exactly how to hold me. After one dance he drifted casually off, saying he might see me later.

Then came the first stage of a drama. A thin bespectacled but quite kindly-looking boy asked me if I wanted to dance. I accepted gratefully, and as we danced we dully talked about O Levels and pop records. He seemed to have a set way of dancing – first just jogging about opposite me, then putting his arms round my waist and leaning back and talking, then going closer and silenter. I felt quite pleasant and dizzy because of the heat and the cider.

After a bit he began to rub his cheek against mine and became rather amorous. I suppose it was hard not to as practically everyone around us was fondling and kissing, not in an awful way but quite light-heartedly. I did not want to, however, as I could not be light-hearted about it, and neither did I really love him. He was pressing closer and closer, and I felt his lips on my cheek, and then on my lips, making a pecking movement, though being lips they felt not peckish but rubbery.

I felt awful and guilty and kept trying to get away from him. I tried every gimmick – I must go upstairs, I must get some food, I must ask my friend something, but always he waited for me, a tense anxious look on his straight-nosed face. I began to feel worse and worse. At one time he asked me if I wanted a 'breather'. I thankfully agreed, only to realise suddenly that this was not an excuse to drift away from him, but a sign that we must go somewhere together. Heavens! To what dark nook, cranny or bedroom would he lead me? I found it was to be outside. He took my hand and we walked down the path. At the end of it I said I was cold so we went back to the stuffy, dim red room.

I managed to wangle Geraldine to say we had to go soon, and at last I could say that this must be the last dance. He seemed to think this called for a vehement display of passion, and kissed me for almost all the dance.

THURSDAY 30 SEPTEMBER

1966

Sometimes I am depressed because there is so much badness in the world, so many people are suffering war even if I am not at the moment, and the world will never get better. Sometimes I am depressed because I feel shut in my little cramped family world in the evenings, where I should be happy but am so often sad and cross, after I had meant to be so good. I often feel terribly alone in the evenings.

But there are always good or nice things in life too. There are the solid comforting nice things like cups of tea, and the lovely things which are not only superficially comforting but really beautiful, like lying in the long grass alone at Grittleton in the sun, looking at the trees and knowing the house is there, and feeling a tangle of happiness because everything is so beautiful. And there are lands sunken in sunny valleys, with hills around, and the wonderful cut-off beauty of mountains where you are in a different world with different cool air and nothing is cramped or petty. Some people say countryside is depressing but I think it is just the opposite. My only fear is that before long it will all be built on – there will be rows of council houses covering that peaceful spot at Grittleton where you can feel so happy. Still, I'm sure the good things in life can't go, even if the countryside is built over. They will still be there in some form or other – if only there wouldn't still be so many bad and depressing things too.

RUSSELL KANE

Russell Kane is a stand-up comedian and actor, who won the coveted Edinburgh Comedy Award in 2010. Born in 1975, he was brought up in Essex where he still lives. Kane has made numerous appearances on TV, including Live at the Apollo, I'm a Celebrity … Get Me Out of Here Now *and* Stupid Man, Smart Phone.

When I was at school, I was only just in the league above the extremely bullied and lonely kids. I just about avoided getting beaten up every day, but I had no real social connections to speak of, and I certainly had no interest from any girls. Writing the diary was my way of dealing with everything I was going through.

At the time of writing this diary I was 13 … going on 11. I was physically and emotionally immature for my age: small, with buck teeth, and a bad haircut from the bloke at Whiskers who gives kids without their mums bad haircuts.

My diary is boring. It's the diary of a working-class boy who had no idea of his place in the world. I wasn't upstairs, in my room, reading books – that didn't happen until I was a lot older. I was just sat, staring at the wall, writing about what I had for breakfast, and how long I boiled my egg for each morning. Looking back now, I'd just like to reassure the younger me that it would all work out OK in the end.

At the front of Russell's diary:
WARNING!
Privacy Factor 8
Unauthorised personel are requested not to turn any further.
If so, you are liable to be prosecuted and receive a criminal
record.
Anyone called James will be personally smashed in.
SIGNED R Kane
Think!

If you've been foolish enough to turn this far, may God help
you.

TUESDAY 3 JANUARY
1989

Russell is 13.

What a day. Got up nice and ... late. Mum said that we'd have
scrambled eggs for lunch, but instead we had awful corned beef
salad. Soon I will become vegetarian – just to see Dad's face.

Lunch was horrible enough, then Mum reminded me it
was haircut day. I hate it. I always hate myself afterwards.
More reasons for Sarah Gibson to think I look like a div. Mum
gave me two quid. I took £8 in case I saw any good records.
I went into Whiskers and can you believe it ... I got the idiot
who gives boys without their mums shit haircuts; and boy, did
I get one. I did buy some house records. When I got home I
had to do the weaving project for textiles. Why weave ... Why?
I ended up throwing it in the air. Oh God. I've got weaving

tomorrow, so I have to finish it tonight. I wonder if Dad will ever finish the kitchen? I wonder what dinner is? I wonder what Sarah Gibson's doing?

WEDNESDAY 4 JANUARY
1989

I fancy Mark's friend Chloe. Not a bad first day back at school. I was conscious of my hair and avoided Sarah Gibson; plus, I think I might be in love with Chloe from Woodford. She came round last night with Mark's sister. We played with the camcorder and I zoomed in on one of her boobs. She called me a 'prick' but I didn't mind. I wonder if I'll ever see her again?

Apart from Sarah Gibson there are no good girls in our school. Actually I'm worried about the fact I don't like any of the girls in our school. I have no love life, and of course, no sex life. I have to get myself a quality bird. I don't think I'm gay, that's one consolation – although Wayne Eglington said my hair was 'queer'.

Miss Levrington approved of my weaving, and we are now starting t-shirt printing. Oh god I FANCY CHLOE!

FRIDAY 6 JANUARY
1989

Can't complain about today. Had crunchy bloody nut cornflakes. Designing clocks in DT. I don't think I am ever going to finish the car.

I still can't stop thinking about Chloe. I wish I could ask her out. I need a new pen. Lee 'borrowed' my pen.

On the way home it was hammering down and Wayne was splashing me. I trod in a massive pile of dog shit. I then had a boring nugget, sweetcorn and chips dinner.

FRIDAY 13 JANUARY
1989

In DT we are designing an implement that can get all of the marmite out of its jar. Had to wait bloody ages for a bus. At the bus stop me and Wayne saw a man pee. *Dallas* started up again. I thought I'd try to follow it, but it is still boring rubbish. Me and my brother tried a ouija board – it doesn't work. I'm going to watch *Poltergeist* tonight, I hope it's good.

TUESDAY 17 JANUARY
1989

I got up at 6.41 to go to school. I had Frosties for breakfast. I then got dressed. I waited for about 15 minutes for a bus. When I got to school Wayne had my jacket for me, it's well cool. The lessons were boring.

Claire Mulley told me that Sarah and Paul were finished, so I asked Claire to ask Sarah for me. She said I'd have to ask her myself. Outside school she ran away.

Please say yes Sarah – I don't think I could take a no.

WEDNESDAY 25 JANUARY

1989

I got up at 6.41 to go to school, I had an egg for breakfast I then got dressed. I waited for about 6 minutes for a bus. When I got to school Wayne was not there yet. The lessons were rubbish as usual.

In German, Lee told me my new bird was fifteen and called Tina. We plan an orgy up at the cinemas next Saturday.

After school Wayne got done. Newman and I went to his bus stop where I was attacked with elastic bands by Barry and Paul White. When I got in I felt really hacked off.

Sod Sarah. Come on Tina.

JEALOUSY

Who is he then?
This man of yours
Is he earthy, rugged, lean
Is he kind, secure – does he speak well
No?
He has then perhaps an excellent sense of humour
Isn't subject to bestial, frail emotion

Who is he then
Your holiday lover
English – no?
Irish perhaps,

For you'd like a real man.
European?
Perhaps another continent
I'm incontinent
With rage

daddy. The phone rang and my mum said "It's your cousin Joanne", and I said to my dad, as a joke, "oh! who's died now!", and it turned out someone had died. Boo, my jokes have bad timin Then I watched "Who's line is it anyway?" with the ever so sexy Greg Prupes & Ryan Styles. A list of my favourite men (friends I mean

Jesus - obviously
Olly - "
Kevin Prosch
Ryan Stiles
Greg Prupes
Ringo Starr - obviously
Paul McCartney
George Harrison
John Lennon
Daddy
Pete
Jesse
Robin

Postman Pat
Paul Elliot
Chris Bowden
Chris Gower
Matt Weeks
Nathan Oley
Luke Lawley
Neil Elliot - hypocrite
(he pulled Sarah Hodgeson - non Christian after telling Robin off for doing it
Gary Wicker

anyway, enough for today, it's 3am!

PIPPA EVANS

Pippa Evans is a musical comedian and improviser, best known for her starring role in the hit improvised musical Showstoppers!, *her appearances on Radio 4 and her sell-out shows at the Edinburgh Festival. She is also the co-founder of the Sunday Assembly, a network of secular congregations around the world. Evans was born in Ealing, west London, in 1982.*

Reading back my diary was fascinating. Oh! the torture of teenage love. I remember this girl who I still carry around with me. Lost in a world of trying to understand spirituality and growing up and FEELINGS.

How similar my love for Olly is to my love for Jesus! Having a teenage crush on a pop star is hard enough, but I decided to go one better and have a crush on our Lord and Saviour, Jesus Christ. I hear he's signing fish down at the local market! Look at his robes! Swoon!

I never could tell Olly how I felt because I knew deep down it wasn't reciprocated. Plus, he was my best friend. So

I never said anything. Classic teen drama stuff! Before I read my diary on Radio 4, I called up Olly and asked if he knew about my crush. 'I knew,' he said, 'but I didn't mind, because no one said anything and so it wasn't a problem. It was all very British.'

I never really mention my three brothers in my diary, or my parents or anyone outside of church-land. I was too busy hanging out with Jesus and my Christian pals. But I am glad I had that space to grow up in, even if I am not a part of it now. It was safe and kind.

How precious to be able to be transported back to a time when I was so sure of something. And to look back 21 years later, knowing that this lost but found little girl is always with me. That we are never truly far away from that part of ourselves we formed in our teenage years. And just so you know, I still love Michael Palin.

TUESDAY 22 JULY

1997

Pippa is 14.

OK, I've been inspired by reading the *Diary of a Teenage Health Freak* to write a diary. I suppose I haven't kept up with other diaries because I got bored. Let's hope this one gets more exciting. OK, so what happened today? Ummm ... well, it's school holidays, so I woke up at 10:18 this morning, and turned on Capital Gold.

I got out of bed and dressed in my mum's old sun dress. It's illuminous green, and it's a no-bra job. I don't know if I like it or not, but it does mean I can get a better suntan!! Anyway, it was really hot, 26°C I think, but I kept finding things to do, so I didn't spend much time outside.

Eleanor rang, she's groovy. Talked to her, then I watched *Neighbours* and *Home and Away*.

Anyway, a gal's diary wouldn't be complete without a long rant about love. Ohhh! At the moment, it's Olly. I mean, it's not like a crush thing. Only, sometimes I think he likes me, and then the next second I think he couldn't care less about me. It's so infuriating. I'm going to this Soul Survivor thing on Friday, and I'm really worried about this Jackie girl. She's been worrying me for ages. I think Olly likes her but I'm not really sure, and now he's had his hair cut, he looks, quite, well, fit, I suppose. Oh! What to do? I know that if God wants me to go out with him, it will happen, but if Olly and Jackie are supposed to go out before us, I don't think I could handle it. It's almost heartbreaking, I feel my heart crease every time he mentions her name, or if someone mentions his name to me. I was really worried because on Sunday he wasn't talking to me and I thought he hated me, but I'm just paranoid, cos I rang him up today and he sounded quite pleased to hear from me, which was nice. I need to pray about it. Help me. Isn't it always when you need God the most, it's almost as if he is furthest away?

WEDNESDAY 23 JULY

1997

I woke up at 9:18 this morning. That's a little too early. I had a shower. I got a letter from this girl Alexia who I went to Germany with last year, and replied immediately as she is leaving for Vietnam next month. Wow! I hope the war has finished.

I posted an entry to the Paul McCartney competition I saw yesterday. I then listened to Monty Python and basically vegged. I made some French toast and felt a bit sick. I cleaned my room. I got rid of the stool that's been bugging me since I moved in here, and tidied my desk and my dressing table. I even sprayed leather protector on my shoes! Man, I was bored. I put up a new Postman Pat poster, as well as the Mr Blobby one Hannah gave me.

I saw *Ten of the Best* on VH1 which was by Paul McCartney. He is up his own bum! Four of his 'Ten of the Best' songs were actually by *him*! I thought that was very arrogant!

I tried to ring Louise C, Sarah and Little Paul, but none of them were in or they were engaged. Why do I have popular friends? I could've rung Olly, he's always in, but I didn't want to crowd him. God told me not to do that, he gave me a picture of a hot air balloon and said that if I want Olly, I mustn't pull on the fraying ropes, or he'll slip away. Oh! Oh! Oh! Why is it so hard?

THURSDAY 24 JULY
1997

Olly gave me a birthday present, Monty Python's *Meaning of Life*, which is great. I wish I could read into the present, but it says on the card 'presents don't mean anything', so I can't, which is a piss pot!!

WEDNESDAY 30 JULY
1997

Hi! Wow, it's been six days! I just got back from my holiday at Shepton Mallet about one hour ago. It was super. I really enjoyed it. Those who went were: Sam, Luke, Nathan, Matt, Mark, Sophie and others. It was groovy. Kevin Prosch, the best Christian music writer ever, was there, and he is excellent. He has a song called 'Wheels' and it is super.

PRAISE THE LORD FOR MY FRIENDS!! BLESS THEM ALL! I really want to tell the people about Jesus, wow! You know what just happened as I wrote that? The album (which I've never listened to before) said 'the Father and the Spirit will protect you from all your fears'. Isn't that awesome? PRAISE GOD!

Ruth and Sarah were supposed to be sharing the tent with me, but because they're so silly, they didn't want to, so they slept in the mini bus, and I had the whole tent to myself! I felt God there so much, his presence was huge. I must have been blessed every day at least once! I wanna ride on the wheel of God. I wanna ride on the wheel of God, yeah!

THURSDAY 7 AUGUST
1997

Woke up at about 10 o'clock. I wrote my thank you letters and posted them. I watched a film – *Big* – with my daddy. The phone rang and my mum said 'it's your cousin, Joanne' and I said to my dad, as a joke, 'oh, who's died now?' and it turned out someone had died. Boo. My jokes have bad timing.

Then I watched *Whose Line is it Anyway?* with the ever so sexy Greg Prupes and Ryan Stiles. A list of my favourite men:

Jesus (obviously)
Olly (obviously)
Kevin Prosch
Ryan Stiles
Greg Prupes
Ringo Starr – obviously
Paul McCartney
George Harrison
John Lennon
Daddy
Postman Pat...

SATURDAY 13 DECEMBER
1997

I met Michael Palin. Here it is in detail:

At 10.05 am I left my house to collect Olivia. We went to Dillons via the Halifax and arrived at 10.30am. I bought *Full Circle* (Michael Palin's book) and we were told to come back at 11.30. We waited outside, and then went inside. At about 12.15pm Michael came up the stairs. He is so beautiful. I suddenly got really excited, and I lost my throat. I said 'hi … hi, my names Pippa' and Olivia butted in. Anyway, Michael said, 'Oh, you're Pippa' and he stuck his hand out to shake my hand. I DIDN'T EVEN HAVE TO ASK! He said 'thank you for your rather forceful letter', and I said 'thank you for your reply' and he said 'yes, you got a letter back, didn't you?' Then he signed my book 'to the wonderful Pippa from your number one fan, Michael Palin'.

WOW.

MONDAY 15 JUNE
1998

My life is a big pile of shit. As you know I have been in love with Olly since the day I met him and haven't stopped loving him since.

However, yesterday my heart was ripped in two when Luke basically said that Olly is on the verge of pulling either Tally or Miriam. Now this made me exceedingly depressed at first, but what made it worse was that this had happened on Saturday night when Olly had told me that I couldn't go to Luke's house. This means he didn't want me there. Also he said that we would go and celebrate the end of exams on Sunday evening after church, but he decided again that he was going to Luke's flat.

Yesterday I was walking through Walpole Park and I cried because I just felt so alone. I ended up at Olivia's house and just cried for 20 years because I felt so miserable. I am just so depressed cos my whole life is falling apart.

I messed up half my exams because I felt miserable because Olly hadn't bothered to ring in two weeks. I feel really fat and really ugly. I just want a boyfriend because I want to know someone loves me. I know I am supposed to only need Jesus's love but it doesn't always work. Jesus can't hug me or kiss me in the same way.

464 - 7891

SONGS IVE WRITTEN

5959	DIFFORD - BARTLETT
SUNDAY	DIFFORD - BARTLETT
WHOS WHO, WHEN IT COMES TO YOU	DIFFORD
DO YOU READ ME?	DIFFORD
ANOTHER YOU ANOTHER ME	DIFFORD - BATCHELOR
WINE AN CHIPS!	DIFFORD
MY WORLD	DIFFORD
AND MAY YOUR	DIFFORD
THE AND AND THE WAS	DIFFORD
DINGO CRUTCH.	DIFFORD
RIO'LA ZOMERSET	DIFFORD
YOU NOSE IT MAKE SENSE (BB)	DIFFORD
CONDUIRE UNE FILLE	DIFFORD
STAR DANCE	DIFFORD
I CANT MAKE SOLUTIONS ANYMORE	DIFFORD
LADY WHITE CLOUDS	DIFFORD.
DO THE DUCH	DIFFORD.
YOU LOOK SO GUILTY IN THAT MACK, MAC.	DIFFORD
FUX! SCORING BIRTH.	DIFFORD. TWINKLE
GOLDEN RAYS AND SOMIC SPEYS	DIFFORD - TWINKLE
TIZER DE BAR	DIFFORD - OTHERS
I AM YOU YOU ARE ME BIRDS OF THE LONELY SEA	DIFFORD.
ALONE AND ME (HARMONY)	DIFFORD
COLARADO KILLER	DIFFORD - SPACER.
HUNGER	J. GILES - DIFFORD
WHOS THAT CAT?	DIFFORD.
UNICORN	DIFFORD - DRISCOLL
BLACK JACK	Captain Chis -
POVENT FILMS	Captain Chis.
So I went	Captain Chis

CHRIS DIFFORD

Chris Difford is a singer, musician, lyricist and record producer, born in Greenwich in 1954. He is a founder member (with writing partner Glenn Tilbrook) of legendary British group Squeeze.

My teenage diaries connect me with that young man who was only focused on one thing – music. Records were bought and played. Wanting to be in a band was everything and playing guitar was an uphill struggle – it still is.

Reading between the lines I can also see a young man hooked on long nights out with his mates getting stoned and drinking cider. I was often on a mission without any destination. Yet I still managed to keep a diary. It was my friend and my companion – it came with me everywhere and my friends often picked it up for a read, and in some cases a scribble. I was happy for people to read my words and see where my head was at. Looking back, I can see the darkness and the adventure in equal measures. At the back of my diary I would chronicle songs I had written and the bands I had seen play live; I also logged phone numbers and even had David Bowie's home number, though I'm not sure how or why.

Each year I would buy or nick a new diary from Boots in Lewisham. It was a pilgrimage like no other, the fresh pages full of possibilities and hope. The old diary – all scruffy and filled with the passing of time, hangovers and affairs – soon to be summoned to the shelf.

My diary was everything. You could say it replaced my teddy at the bedside, and inside there are so many lovely memories that I can still smell to this day when I open it up to read its mostly illegible handwriting.

Today I keep a blog on my website. It's not the same as the pen or pencil slanted over the page. It's not as personal when you type the words onto the screen. Not so witty or open to interpretation. You just can't beat a diary.

MONDAY 14 JANUARY

1974

Chris is 19.

Work was ok. Had a bath and went over to Glenn's and we just sat and played tapes. What a laugh it was. Wrote some lyrics and came home.

I am at a crisis point – my ego is intoxicating me. I reckon I'll have to stop it before it ruins me. It keeps asking questions and then answering them. I feel so confused.

TUESDAY 12 MARCH

1974

Feel really ill. Like death warmed up. Bought the double Beatles Album. Went to bed this afternoon. Kept collapsing on the floor. Made it over to No 4. Glenn pissed me off. Effing cat had a stroke. Went up to London to play to Tony, Mike and John Leyton. I was a like a wreck but just managed to scrape through two and a half hours' songs. Felt worse as time went on. Who cared? I reckon that if things don't change then I feel like splitting from Glenn and the rest of them. He could do it better on his own anyway. I can't see this lasting. Good night.

FRIDAY 12 APRIL
1974

Good Friday. Had a bath and Jools [*Jools Holland, Chris's friend*] drove me down to Benenden in Kent on his motor machine. Really nice fast long ride along the A21. Lost my sunglasses. Went to the pub in the evening – got chucked out cos of my studded leather jacket. Dear oh dear. Jools is a really mad driver.

SUNDAY 14 APRIL
1974

Got up, cleaned up. Came home to London on the bike with Jools. As we got into London we got stopped by the pigs. And they took us to the nick and we got charged. Jools is 16 – no licence and no tax, no MOT and no insurance – and me, for aiding and abetting. Sad but true. So wheeled the bike to Jools's and watched *Yellow Submarine*.

TUESDAY 16 APRIL
1974

Dear Chris
Look here. It's all blown up out of proportion yeah? Mummy and Daddy don't want you to be a popstar. God, what a word! I lost my love for Hatty but still like to love Jo. Also there are other problems which can't be put into words. I cried and

I'll cry again because love is the way I feel. The Chauffeur of words driving them around and around my head. The people I have hurt have helped me – in a way I could thank them. I am not sad. Because I am happy. Sitting here behind my long face. Watching everybody's every move. Seeing how people react and how they don't. And now the chauffeur feels terrified of tomorrow. I can't love you, so please hurt me, so I can forget you and carry on.

Love Chris.

THURSDAY 25 APRIL

1974

I am fully nude and writing this. Well, today saw the birth of our new Rock and Roll band. We rehearsed from 3 until midnight. John Leyton our manager paid us – we got £5 each – our first wage as a group. Band Name – 'The Kids'.

TUESDAY 25 JUNE

1974

Went up to Biba in London for a job and got it – as a porter of goods out back. I start Monday – £28 per week. It's only for two weeks so that's ok.

Met Nicky and her sister. We went down the pub and she kissed me more tonight. I really would like to know where I stand. I was gonna buy her a Marc Bolan LP today but money can't buy love. Tell me: where do I stand? Are we still hard hugging Squeezers full of love? What's the truth? Anyone else who reads this, read on and see the next episode. Meanwhile, don't be so bloody nosey – this is my secret record of my life. This is my list of close friends who could read this if they ask: Nicky. Glenn. Max. Eric. Mark. And that's all.

THURSDAY 27 JUNE
1974

Got up early again but that's work. Broke the whole lift circuit – Oh boy. Still, came home and Jools was here so we went for a pleasant evening in the pub. I rang Nicky – I should have gone babysitting with her but I didn't and that's tough. She loves Kenny anyway so why worry? Doubt she ever loved me. If you read this Nicky, don't you think it's strange? All that lovey dovey stuff early on??

FRIDAY 28 JUNE
1974

Work was okay. Got me pay. Jools got a job at Biba today playing piano, the talented lucky sod. But it's good, so three of us at Biba now. So came home and Nicky came over and the rest of us went down the pub. She didn't. We said Goodbye. I am single again. Must get a girl. But I love Nicky.

WEDNESDAY 3 JULY

1974

Went over to Glenn's. But his stepdad threw me out – he got very stroppy and called me a bum. So I was left on the street. Second time I've been chucked out this week. Where does one go? Well I am ok and sleeping at Jools's. But where will the man with suitcases go tomorrow?

TUESDAY 30 JULY

1974

Went over to my mum's house. She says I can move back in there but will it just be the same as before? I'm very mixed up right now. What with music, lyrics ... and girls of course.

WEDNESDAY 25 SEPTEMBER

1974

Good news – Island want us to go on the road before we record and when we have, the doors are open – which sounds good. Went out for a booze with Jools, Keith and my old school mate Eric. Really nice night it was.

I reckon the band are the best bunch of guys I have ever met. They really are getting a whole lot of fun. I could never leave. I sort of love them. We all know each other so well and it's making days seem brighter for me.

THURSDAY 17 JULY

1975

The group Squeeze might be doing things soon one way or another. We play the Marquee soon – that should be a good break for us. Lots of important ears will be there to hear us or so I hear.

Music means so much to me. It says everything I ever feel. There must be a song for every feeling I ever have. Without music, life would be pretty empty. I hope I write songs for somebody's feelings. I've just lit my second fag and my last in this pub. All I need to do now is face the music and later face love. I so often get them mixed up. Other guys don't get in so much trouble. This book is like a friend. You can tell it everything.

We are going to rehearse, go on the road and then record. Band are all in a good mood, even Paul. Perhaps one day I'll be able to look back on this page and remember how it all began.

And now for the future – maybe there will be a line-up change. Obviously Glenn and me remain founder members of the band as we write all the songs. Jools and Paul are pretty fab. Squeeze begin their life ...

MONDAY 29 SEPTEMBER

1975

I'D LIKE to sail around the world, visit the Far East, swim in the coral sea, fly across Russia, have six records in the top twenty. Be photographed by David Bailey. Write a novel. Act in a Stanley Kubrick film with Mr McDowell. Meet Elvis Presley and Mr Bowie. Sky dive in Hampshire. Have a house in Paris, Somerset and Beverly Hills. Walk from John O Groats to Land's End. Drive a fast car. Drink with Frank Sinatra or Dean Martin. Wear nice clothes. Give my baby a birthday. Ride a horse in Mexico. Eat at The Ritz. Have my very own film unit. Kick sand in Mike Cooper's face ...

I'D HATE to be dragged along by a Rolls Royce. Thrown off a high building. Starve. Not to have six singles in the top twenty. Not to be in love. Glenn to be killed, my child to die at birth. Ride a motorbike backwards, meet Bob Dylan or Tom Jones. Sit in a burning house. Be eaten alive by spiders. To dream bad things. Live in London all my life. Ride in the back of a funeral car. Sing my songs to monks or nuns. My hair to fall out. My right hand to drop off. Religion to get in my life. Walk backwards up a hill. To ever see Mike Cooper again in my life.

wasn't leaving so soon, I'm just getting
into it in a major way.
2·00 pm, met David + Jeep + set off
for the sheep farm by the Jordan.
Rode, swam, talked, rode, rounded
up sheep, ate peanut butter
sandwiches + drank tea by the river.
Rode until after sunset then
herded in the sheep-saw loch.
Ate prickly pears. I'm beginning to
become be addicted to this outdoor
life.

August 27th
Ai was picking with us today. Jeremy
in the Negev, alas. I can't look
into his twinkly brown eyes.
It was enjoying picking today. Ai
reviled Horace + Peter bored us
by saying how the Ulpan lot had

RACHEL
JOHNSON

Rachel Johnson was born in London in 1965. She is a novelist, diarist, journalist and broadcaster, former editor of the Lady *and a regular columnist in the* Mail on Sunday *and* The New European.

I first started writing a diary on 29 September 1973. It began, 'I am just eight' (it was three weeks after my birthday). I kept it going for a record three days, as on the third day my older brother almost died of peritonitis. 'I have got a blocked nose and a cold,' I recorded, putting myself front and centre as is the writer's wont. 'Alex has got apendisitist.' (Alexander or Al is the family name for Boris.) My diary petered out for good at Christmas with the words, 'Hate, hate! I'm never going to write this again.' After that, I wrote entries only when my mother forced us to keep daily diaries on family holidays abroad as teenagers.

We went to Maine in 1982. Every day my little brother Jo carefully wrote 'Lobsters In Maine' at the top of each page every day and then laid aside his pen, devoid of inspiration.

On foreign trips as a teenager and student I filled notebooks. I can't think why, but I'm glad I did now as there is a record for posterity of my memorable six-week spell on a kibbutz in Galilee in my 'gap year' with Alexander/Boris. On re-reading it's revealing. I am always going off looking for him to do things, but then feel I'm not interesting enough, while he spouts Horace in apple orchards. My keen interest in male company shines through, as does my concern with my weight, my paranoid self-pity and my interest in food (some things never change). I'm amazed that as an adult I've had two volumes of diaries published. You'd never guess from reading my childhood and teenage diaries that I had it in me.

TUESDAY 7 AUGUST

1984

Rachel is 18.

Flight delayed one hour. Tel Aviv/Belfast desks at Gatwick tucked away in an inconspicuous part of ground floor. Lots of families going to Tel Aviv – not so many businessmen in evidence except for smoothie in a cream suit who was irritated with Al and me for failing to understand how the lift worked.

Our hand luggage was searched endlessly. Al was spotted and was thoroughly frisked by a security officer. I'm sure it was his crumpled seersucker jacket.

I'm writing this lying on my 'bed' in my room at Kfar Hanassi. In a way it was just what I expected – shabby corrugated iron sheds, small cement huts (I'm inhabiting one), a large swimming pool, floodlit tennis court, dining hall, small library (subterranean), lots of dark-skinned slender Israelis/European/Anglo Saxon Jews around the place. I must stop asking people if they are Jewish – of course they are. I feel like an imposter and certainly look like one.

Al is living in utter squalor with two others – I'm living with a Sarah from Maida Vale. Seems fine, been here a couple of days.

Ate in dining hall. Yoghurt, cream cheese and bread, tomatoes. Delicious.

Al and I wandered around vaguely after that, found a weight training room, the schwimmbad. He was low – nauseating room and obviously idle and untidy roommates. Said 'two to three weeks max here'. I really hope this goes all right. I must aim to do some classics, manage the obviously huge workload, get brown, be dynamic, talk to people. I'm very tired. 7.30 rise. No work tomorrow.

WEDNESDAY 8 AUGUST

1984

Very hot – searing light – I must get some sunglasses. Had breakfast with Al – rather depressing for some reason. Does he think I drag him down or what? Anyway, we were presently joined by a blond window-cleaner called Jonathan.

I worked for a bit. Old gardener who looked like Moses approached and started burbling about how sad it was when volunteers didn't keep up their gardens – looking pointedly at the scrubby plot at my feet.

Did nothing much this afternoon – was savouring those last moments of freedom. Work starts tomorrow at 6am, breakfast is at 8.30, then countless more hours. I'm in the factory, which has two sections, the Graveyard and Hell. I trust I'll survive. Supper was the same as last night.

Am in bed, swabbing torn heel. Oh! what will the morrow bring?

I'd better start writing on both sides.

THURSDAY 9 AUGUST

1984

At 5 to 6 set off in the early dawn light towards the Factory. Nobody had specified which part, where, whom, etc. I wandered around the building asking Arabs if they spoke any English, where I should go and other vital questions. I came across Bob, who told me to go to Chaim-Ka, in another building.

I waited on a packing case in the shade and watched the sun climb above the trees. NB Israel had no trees at all. JNF [*Jewish National Fund*] planted every single one by hand. It is forbidden to cut them down.

Chaim-Ka appeared at 6.40 and gave me into the hands of Mossie, who is in charge of the valve shop.

So I sat at a desk and lubricated screws, then screwed them into holes in valves along with seats, washers and nuts and then plonked in ball bearings.

Breakfast and break. Rejected brown-tinged hard boiled egg, drank coffee, next to Collette.

Work continued much as usual. 10.00 tea break. Outside in heat. 12.00 lunch. Saw Al, looked gloomy, 12pm–3pm more valves.

Swam and lay in sun till 4. Tried to sleep. Meeting at 5.30. Got work clothes, new boots, ate bread and peanut butter.

Went to supper. Then went to the TV room in search of Al. He was there watching the Olympics.

FRIDAY 10 AUGUST
1984

Got up with slightly more alacrity today, and walked through the empty kibbutz to the factory. Sarah didn't wake me up this morning – or perhaps I slept through her noise. I have to admit it was quite depressing getting up so early. Mossie told me to make some tea for myself which I did and then started on the valves again.

Lunch, having showered and changed my clothes. Am getting v bored of the volunteers. They seem so stupid. Read, swam, lay in the sun. Did some Virgil.

Afterwards I found Al in the coffee place drinking coffee. We decided that the kibbutz was fine. It's better for Al because he's got all his work to do whereas I have to make more effort socially to feel that it's all worthwhile. It is an effort when you don't really like the other volunteers. I'm in the Institute waiting for the pub to open. Then I will brave it and have a drink. Al bloody better come with me.

Al didn't come so I went by myself. The pub is housed in a temporarily disused air raid shelter. Drinks are amazingly cheap – about 80 shekels – 25p – and they give generous measure. Nick and Tony and I were the only volunteers to begin with – it was mainly Kibbutzniks. Had good talk with Tony about Oxford. Susan spilt her vodka and orange over my white cheesecloth culottes at around 11.00 so I decided to call it a day.

SATURDAY 11 AUGUST

1984

Slept heavily. Awoke feeling ghastly at 11.00, couldn't get up. At 11.30 went to the Institute and saw Al, who gave out a particularly liquid and nauseating burp which I felt sure would make me throw up. I went into the evil smelling ladies and tried unsuccessfully. Collapsed in bed feeling ghastly, fingertips and arms throbbing.

WEDNESDAY 22 AUGUST

1984

Day off.

Slept till 8.30, ate huge amounts of toast and margarine, read the paper then sunned and swam, while talking to Aran and David (Israeli shepherd). David asked me to go down to the Jordan with him and I 'assented eagerly'. Ate lunch and then lazed around till 3pm. As I walked towards the jeep I realised I was wearing completely the wrong clothes. I'd forgotten he'd talked about riding. We drove in the jeep down to the Jordan valley where the sheep were grazing. V hot and dry. Got out, drank some water, stopped by the orchard and picked some apples for supper. I groomed Mandy my horse, then we mounted and walked towards the Jordan. I was riding Western style which I found very easy. It was v bucolic to be outside of the bloody valve factory. By the swimming hole in the Jordan was an Orthodox family who were shocked when Roy the sheepdog sprang into their Citroen. David and I thought it was v funny. I stripped off, aware of my relative nudity compared to the Orthodox family, who swam in shirts and dresses and hats. We went for a half hour ride, then rounded up the sheep, Kfar Hanassi's Merino flock. David rides, swims beautifully. Talks a bit too much with an Israeli accent and a lisp. We had peanut butter sandwiches on a rock, then we did more herding with David galloping off over the horizon shouting orders like 'herd up those on that hill', he's got an upper-class English accent when he shouts.

We got in the sheep, brushed down the horses and then raced back to catch supper, which we missed.

Fed sick lambs from a bottle. One was dead which was quite a shock. By this time it was 9pm, showered, changed, and went to the pub. Then to bed – 4.45 rise tomorrow for orchards.

FRIDAY 24 AUGUST
1984

4am. Went to orchards. I've made Reuven and the others love me by various subtle ploys and suckings-up. Jeremy is bloody sexy as far as I'm concerned. Picked apples furiously until 8.00, breakfast, grits, toast, cottage cheese. I wish I wasn't leaving so soon, I'm just getting into it in a major way.

2pm. Met David and set off for the sheep farm by the Jordan. Rode, swam, talked, rode, rounded up sheep, ate peanut butter sandwiches and drank tea by the river. Rode until after sunset then herded in the sheep. Ate prickly pears. I'm beginning to become addicted to this outdoor life.

MONDAY 27 AUGUST
1984

Al was picking with us today. Jeremy isn't here – alas. I can't look into his twinkly brown eyes. It was crippling picking today. Al recited Horace. Breakfast, and Reuven announced that since we had finished the apples we weren't going back. Back to uncle Mossie in the valve shop I went. Put valves together for a couple of hours, then abandoned ship and lay in bed, dreaming of Jeremy. Lay by pool, saw Jeremy's wife – skinny bitch.

Later on went out to Jordan with David and the sheep. Starry starry night. David had made a fire, steaks, Turkish coffee, and pitta. We lay on blankets next to the horses and two dead sheep and giggled for a couple of hours. It was quite difficult not to put my hand out and touch him. I restrained myself.

TUESDAY 28 AUGUST
1984

Sat with shepherds at supper. Afterwards I decided that it was silly for me to leave the Kibbutz as I was enjoying it so much and was just starting to know people. So Al and I went off to see Alec and Edna where I broached the subject of me staying on after the 10th for a few weeks. They seemed delighted but my ticket might pose a problem.

ROBERT WEBB

Robert Webb is a writer, actor and comedian, born in Lincolnshire in 1972. He met David Mitchell while they were both students at Cambridge, and they went on to make the cult sitcom Peep Show *and the sketch show* That Mitchell and Webb Look. *Webb has also written the best-selling memoir* How Not to Be a Boy.

Harriet Jaine, producer of My Teenage Diary: Robert Webb's diary is raw, edgy, hilarious, painfully honest and gut-wrenchingly sad. It shines an uncompromising spotlight onto the frequently appalling experience of being a teenager.

First and foremost, this is a writer's diary – in the very first entry, the young Robert is given an electric typewriter by his mum for his seventeenth birthday. From then on, from his bedroom in a bungalow in Lincolnshire, we can feel Webb testing out the power of words and finding out that language can take the cruelty of the world and make it funny … 'Whether this is a difficult time or whether life will always be this painful, I don't know. To write it all down is a way of finding out.'

And this diary is extremely funny. From foolishly getting off with the wrong girl at a party in the village hall to having a crush on a co-worker at a supermarket – Webb takes his worst, most foolish teenage moments and turns them into brilliant bits of black comedy. Listening to him sarcastically reading out extracts during recording – and watching him wince at his teenage writing style – was one of the funniest experiences I've had making the show.

Heartbreakingly, the very worst thing then does actually happen: Robert's mother dies very suddenly from lung cancer. And the description of the journey to her funeral, as his brother fades out Kylie Minogue on the car stereo out of respect for the occasion, is one of the most unflinching bits of observation in any diary, anywhere. Comedy and tragedy walk hand in hand, and this diary is a perfect example of that.

SEPTEMBER

1989

Rob is 16.

I suppose the desire is just to get everything down on paper
and try and learn from it. I've often thought: 'One day I'm
going to look back on my later teenage years as a rather
difficult period of my life.' Well that's the hypothesis – here
comes the experiment! Whether this *is* a difficult time or
whether life will always be this painful, I don't know. To write
it all down is a way of finding out. I'm a hopeless nostalgic
of course, and presume this will always be true of me. So
assuming this journal survives a few years, then it will
probably be of massive sentimental value one day. I simply
can't imagine myself older than 25. What will it be like?

All week Mum had been trying to get me excited about
my birthday present and as usual, she succeeded. In the end
it was an incredibly amazing electric typewriter. OK, driving
lessons would have been more useful, but this shows that she
recognises my interests and that's worth more to me.

But the event that really caused repercussions was my
17th birthday piss-up in the Angel. Look, I wasn't that pissed,
just rather squiffed that's all. Anyway the upshot is that I get
off with both Debbie and Sarah K. And here's where the shit
hits the fan: the following days afterwards the situation is this.

Debbie has decided she fancies me and gets Jane
Woodthorpe to try and get me to go out with her (Debbie that
is, not Jane). Though I like her, Debbie is unfortunately not
the subject of my attention or – let's face it – lust. That is most
definitely Sarah's job and over that weekend I most foolishly

allowed myself to fall in love with the idea of going out with her. Well, although I never asked her myself she got wind of my intentions and politely said 'sod off' and promptly went out with Mike Mason instead. I speak light of it now but at the time it was flipping devastating and I plunged heroically into a week-long depression session.

Let's not mistake: I don't get pissed off for a week just because of one girl (who in the cold light of logical appraisal doesn't come out very favourably anyway). No, what got to me was the regularity with which this seemed to be occurring. How many girls in the 5 years up till then had eventually said 'Let's just be friends'? Sarah J, Maddy, Gill, Meg, Bridget, now Sarah K. As I said in a letter to Maddy: 'I should have known it would screw up. It always has screwed up. It always will screw up.' What didn't exactly help matters was that Maddy then started going out with Andrew Plater. Andrew who?! What a shock that was. 'He's so cute' she says. Hmm, yes, cute, funny, blond hair and works at Gateway supermarket – sounds a little familiar to me. I *must* be imagining things …

Anyway, Andrew is of course mates with Mike 'I'm a twat and I steal women' Mason and so a cosy little foursome has now developed from which bachelor Rob is now coldly excluded.

It suddenly struck me that I was alone, very alone, and that's where the rot set in. Everywhere I look, everyone has someone. I mean I wouldn't mind if I was flipping boring, stupid and repulsively ugly. But I'm not and it pisses me off that people like Sarah see more in people like Mike Mason than in me. Frankly, what does he have that I don't? Experience and luck, that's what. Is that it? Have I just been unlucky? I don't know. Quite frankly I don't have a flipping clue.

MONDAY 23 OCTOBER
1989

Last Saturday was Ben's party at Carrington village hall.
Danced mostly but then – shit! – got off with Debbie again.
Oh balls, what an idiot. I even told her I'd give her a ring! I'm
in some doubt. I mean I don't *really* fancy her. She's pleasant
enough but I just don't think there's enough attraction for me
there. Maybe I'm being too fussy. Maybe that's what's been
wrong in the past and she's just what I need.

FRIDAY 17 NOVEMBER
1989

Update: Sid's party, the most hyped spectacle since *Batman*. I
was talking to Billy and Aaron when Debbie kind of connected
herself to me. Well we sat down and well ... what could I do
but get off with her? It was only briefly and I suddenly realised
that I didn't want this situation at all. There was a party going
on and I didn't want to be sat there, annoyed, with someone
I don't find remotely attractive. Anyway, after just one fairly
long kiss, I heard 'U Got the Look' come on and said 'Oh I've
just got to dance to this.' She relented reluctantly and we went
to dance. Well, already on the floor was Sarah K who I fancy
LIKE SHITTING HELL. And then I did something rather
despicable. I started dancing exclusively AT Sarah, totally
ignoring Debbie. As well as holding all my sexual attention,
Sarah is also a cool mover and we really started FREAKING.
After 3 or 4 songs it became clear to Debbie that she might

want to go and do something else. I felt quite guilty of course but didn't really dwell on it.

Dancing with Sarah like that was the most fun I've ever had. It was really varied and sexy and just FUN to do. After a while we went outside to cool off. We didn't get off with each other (obviously more her preference than mine) but really that's not what I expected and I wasn't really disappointed at all.

We split up when we got back inside and I was just going back to talk to everyone when flipping DEBBIE sidles up, shoves a Bacardi and Coke in my face and says: 'I bought you this.' Oh FLIP OFF! I mean hadn't she got the message by now? OK, getting off with her had been a bloody huge mistake; it was leading her on and I suppose she has a right to think me a bit of a shit. But bloody hell, she went RIGHT over the top. She tried to put her arms around me but I just disentangled myself and haven't looked her in the eye all week. I was seriously wondering how I ever could have contemplated going out with her but the answer is simple: DESPERATION. Seventeen and a virgin. Of course it's not just the sex ... but that fact IS the most clear demonstration of my lack of success in relationships.

FRIDAY 24 NOVEMBER 1989

There's a girl at Gateway called Jo who I really fancy. She's quite small with long, dark, wavy hair and a lovely smile. Trouble is she only works on a Saturday and she's always on checkout so I never get to talk to her. Tomorrow night loads of the lower sixth are going to the Angel and I've decided to ask her to come. Well I say 'decided', I mean the likelihood is that I a) won't get the opportunity or b) will chicken out. I keep remembering how bad it was when other girls said no, either down the phone or through other people and how much more embarrassing it would have been if I'd asked them face to face. I think she is much more likely to say yes if I say it myself but that doesn't make it any easier. Anyway, we'll see ...

SATURDAY 25 NOVEMBER
1989

She wasn't at work! AAAAARGH!

SUNDAY 10 DECEMBER
1989

The next Saturday caused the biggest crisis since Sarah. That morning – the inevitable disaster. Maria told me Jo was going out with someone and was 'really head over heels in love with him'. It really was a kick in the balls. You'd think I might be used to it by now but no. I spent the rest of that day, and that week, in a sack of shit.

That week would have been bad enough anyway. Maddy told me that Katy Marsden had said behind my back something I had suspected for years. That I'm basically too funny. Too funny to be taken seriously by girls. 'I like his face and that, but he's always joking. He's just a joke.' Yes, well you Katy Marsden are a scruffy Neneh Cherry-hating racist flipper so you can shove that up the angry little cock you've probably got hiding under your bullshit ballgowns. Is that funny enough for you Katy? Are we chuckling yet, you lumpen, bad-perm, thought-*1984*-was-by-Rudyard Kipling spaz?

SATURDAY 3 MARCH

1990

My concern for Mum deepens. I'm ashamed to realise that this is the first reference in this diary to worrying about anyone but myself. I suppose this book was meant to be about me but it's pathetic all the same. Mum has been in hospital since last Friday with what was supposed to be a chest infection. In fact she has a few cancerous cells on her lung. She might have to have chemotherapy. Jesus Christ I'm so worried. I love her so much. I must resolve to be less selfish, to talk to her about things more often. Life without her is unthinkable, literally unthinkable.

TUESDAY 3 APRIL

1990

Maria finished with Edmund. We seemed to be getting on very well on the bus home today . . .

Found out for sure the week before last that Mum is definitely not going to recover. They say she has about 4 months. I don't want to talk about it, even to you.

TUESDAY 17 APRIL
1990

Derek was ill this morning. Mum's condition gets worse. I feel helpless to do anything. She's dying. I'm not ready for any of this shit.

MONDAY 23 APRIL
1990

Dr Campbell says 48 hours at the most. Mark, Andrew and I were in the front room – he addressed his remarks to the older boys like I was a kid in a nappy in the corner. Christ I want it to be all over. Is that bad of me?

TUESDAY 24 APRIL
1990

Mum dies at 2.45pm. I love you. Sometimes it snows in April.

TUESDAY 1 MAY
1990

Well in the words of many relatives and friends: 'life goes on, doesn't it?' Well yes, for some of us it does. I shouldn't knock it – what the hell do I expect them to say? The funeral was a real highlight. I don't have a suit so I unpicked the badge from my conveniently black sixth form blazer. So a couple of hours later I'd at least taught myself to sew. How's that for silver linings? Mark drove, with me next to him behind the hearse. He was obviously a bit tense, keeping it between second and third gear with the clutch on his Astra squeaking with every change. He said, 'How about a bit of music?' and turned on the radio. It was Kylie Minogue singing 'I Should Be So Lucky'. We endured about 15 seconds of this before he said, 'Yeah, maybe not appropriate.' And then, rather wonderfully, he didn't just turn the radio off; he gently turned the volume down to silence, fading Kylie's warbling out as in respect for the occasion. It occurred to me that this was the single most hilarious thing I'd ever seen or heard. But we all just stared unsmilingly ahead and I tucked it away for later. What's that Graham Greene says about every writer having a shard of glass in his heart? I've got a shard or two in mine now. Mark, fading Kylie out … I've never loved him more. Faces are even grimmer than I expected, especially when they see me. But they're all old. And they don't have what I have. I've got a school badge in my pocket.

I'm overwhelmed with the amount of work I've got to catch up with. But I'll do it. I'm going to Cambridge and nothing's going to stop me. We know who the first person to agree with that kind of talk would be, don't we? Right, well come on then! I wrote in these very pages 'life without her is unthinkable'. Well think it, boy, because it's happened and how can I be afraid of a few poxy A levels when I've gone through this? Never. *I shall win.* Let's say it again but this time mean it: life goes on.

ACKNOWLEDGEMENTS

Thank you to all the people who have helped to make *My Teenage Diary* a success. To Rufus Hound – a matchless host, collaborator and friend. To the completely indispensable Jerry Peal and Kev Mathew, who have recorded the programme since day one with such professionalism and good humour, and to Jerry again for your brilliant editing and Charlotte Hamilton for your delicious lunches. To the team at Talkback – Sharon Fuller, Andrea Gordon, Rebecca Porter, Jonno Richards and Leon Wilson – thank you for all your help and support. To Julie Kaye and Tessa Devonshire – it wouldn't have been possible without your attention to detail and hard work. To Cat Ledger: what did we get ourselves into? To Victoria Payne, the brilliant producer who first came up with the idea and got it commissioned at Radio 4. To Ged Parsons for all your fantastic work script-editing and writing on the radio series. Caroline Raphael and Sioned Wiliam, our two commissioning editors at Radio 4, for your guidance, encouragement and trust. Dan Dearlove and the team at The Backyard Comedy Club for being so accommodating and welcoming to our audiences. Thank you to the team at BBC Books – Yvonne Jacob and Beth Wright – for your patience and help with putting this book together. Susie Hall for your excellent advice on the book jacket design. But the biggest thank you of all goes to the diarists themselves – an amazing group of people who have trusted me with their precious teenage diaries and worked with me to put this book together. It's been a delight and a privilege – thank you!

Samira Ahmed

Rachel Johnson

Sara Pascoe

Chris Difford

Lionel Shriver

Pippa Evans